My Heart Will Go On

OTHER TITLES BY JOY SWIFT

Goodbye Forever? A Mother's Search for Hope
When Death Isn't Fair: Coping With Overwhelming Grief

My Heart Will Go On

An unspeakable crime and
a terrible disease claimed
the lives of Joy's five
children. But that's not
the end of the story.

JOY SWIFT

From the author of *"They're All Dead, Aren't They"*

Pacific Press® Publishing Association
Nampa, Idaho
Oshawa, Ontario, Canada
www.pacificpress.com

Designed by Eucaris L. Galicia
Cover photo from GoodSalt.com

Additional copies of this book are available by calling toll free
1-800-765-6955 or visiting http://www.adventistbookcenter.com.

Unless otherwise noted, all scriptures are quoted from the NIV, the Holy
Bible, New International Version, copyright © 1973, 1978, 1984 by the International Bible Society. Used by permission of Zondervan Bible Publishers.

Scripture quotations attributed to the NKJV are from the Holy Bible, New
King James Version, copyright © 1979, 1980, 1982 by Thomas Nelson, Inc.
Used by permission.
Scripture quotations attributed to the NASB are from the New American
Standard Bible, copyright © 1960, 1962, 1963, 1968, 1971, 1972, 1973,
1975, 1977 by The Lockman Foundation. Used by permission.

Library of Congress Cataloging-in-Publication Data

Swift, Joy.
My heart will go on : an unspeakable crime and a terrible disease claimed the
lives of Joy's five children : but that's not the end of the story/Joy Swift
p.cm.
ISBN 0-8163-2069-1
1. Swift, Joy. 2. Seventh-day Adventists—United States—Biography. 3. Parents of murder victims—United States—Biography. 4. Children—Death—
Religious aspects—Christianity. I. Title.

BX6193.S95A3 2005
248.8'66'092—dc22
[B]   2004060767

05 06 07 08 09 • 5 4 3 2 1

DEDICATION

To my children—Sandy, Matt, and Cody—
who have lived in the shadow of their siblings far too long.
Never forget the part you have played in my healing.
I could not have made it without you.

—Mom

CONTENTS

CHAPTER 1
ONE FATAL NIGHT

He lies in wait near the villages; from ambush he murders the innocent,
watching in secret for his victims (Psalm 10:8).

September 15, 1977, was the night that changed my life. That was the night that I became a victim to a crime more brutal than I could ever have imagined. A crime committed by a fourteen-year-old neighbor boy named Billy Dyer, a boy I had taken into my heart and my home. A boy who played with my children right up to the hour that he took their lives.

My husband, George, and I had gone out for the evening. Thursday night was Bingo night at the American Legion Hall. We had left our four healthy children home alone under the care of our fourteen-year-old son, Steve. Greg was twelve; Tonya, three; and Baby Stacy, just seventeen months old.

Our oldest daughter, Stephanie, was in a hospital dying of cancer. We had spent every extra moment the previous three weeks at her bedside, watching the life drain from her seventeen-year-old body. We needed this evening out to put Stephanie's illness aside briefly and just have fun before picking up the burden once more.

Less than an hour after we kissed the children goodbye, all four lay dead from multiple gunshot wounds to the head and chest. Tonya had also been beaten and stabbed.

George and I arrived home to find ambulances and police cars lining both sides of the gravel road. Though we tried to force our way into the house to be with our children, we were denied access. Instead, we were put into a patrol car and taken to the police station. For the next seven hours we were separated as we endured interrogations, strip searches, powder residue tests, fingerprints, and mug shots. We were suspects in the killings of our own children. It was an intensely angry night.

By morning, the police realized they had no evidence to hold us. They released us with orders not to leave town until notified, and they put us up in a local motel.

The next day Billy Dyer was taken into custody, along with a twenty-year-old accomplice named Ray Richardson, Jr., who had agreed to give Billy a ride to our house and help him commit the crime in exchange for guns and knives Billy intended to steal from our home. Our family was Billy's first target in an intended killing spree to "kill a whole bunch of people until we got caught."

Four innocent children were murdered that horrible night, but many more victims were left alive to cope with the tragedy and deal with indescribable grief.

Not all of us were able to bear the grief. Stephanie found it impossible to fight the cancer and the grief too. Twenty days after her brothers and sisters were killed, Stephanie lost the battle, and we laid her to rest beside them.

In the weeks and months that followed, George and I learned to adjust to life without the children. Being victims changed us. Slain with the children were all our hopes and dreams—for their future and ours—because we couldn't imagine living the rest of our lives without them. Slain also was any shred of trust or security we might have had. We couldn't trust anybody now. No longer could we walk naively through life smelling the roses. Life was too fragile, too vulnerable. If the children could lose their lives so quickly, so could we.

Over time the damage done to our hearts finally healed, but we were both left terribly scarred. We were victims. There was nothing we could do to change what had happened and no way to recover what we had lost.

But we did have some control over what would happen to us in the future. We both vowed that we would not fall victim to anyone or anything ever again. From that point on, every thought, every action, was motivated by self-preservation. We might go down, but we would go down valiantly, kicking and fighting all the way.

For years we grieved together. Unlike many couples who lose a child, we hung tightly to each other and refused to let go. We were all we had, and we would not lose each other. Our greatest fear was that death would snatch one of us away, leaving the other completely alone.

Over the course of several years we developed a relationship with our heavenly Father and learned that we could lean on Him for strength and comfort and, ultimately, for answers to our deepest pain. But we were still victims because we refused to allow ourselves to be anything else.

We had three more children, all born victims of the terrible tragedy that had befallen our family before they were even born. We taught them to depend only on the family and God because no one else in the world could be trusted not to hurt them.

They grew to be strong and independent, trusting in their own ability to care for themselves and to work hard for whatever they needed. They left home to pursue their dreams in the cruel world that could not be trusted. They carried a fire in their hearts that told them they would not fall victim to anyone. They would go down fighting. But like us, they, too, were still victims of the past.

For twenty years George and I grieved for the ones we lost. And then one day I realized that I didn't have to be a victim anymore, not to the future or to the past. In Jesus Christ I could be a victor, if only I would choose to be. I could stand as a victor even over the past. I could not change what happened. But in Christ, I could win the victory over it.

Today I am a victor, and I will stand as a victor for all eternity—all because of one Man from the little town of Nazareth. He is the difference between my being a victim and being a victor. He was both—and so am I.

I write this book for all the people who remain victims of past circumstances. Whether you have been a victim of a terrible crime, of unspeakable abuse, or whatever circumstance beyond your control, there is One who holds the key to release you from the bondage that has held you victim. I stand as a witness to all that we do not have to be held hostage for the rest of our lives. We can break free and stand as victors instead. In the pages that follow, I will tell you how God helped me to become a victor.

CHAPTER 2
VICTIMS LIKE US

The Son of Man must be delivered into the hands of sinful men,
be crucified and on the third day be raised again (Luke 24:7).

I sat in a motel room alone in the dark, feeling worthless and hopeless and devastated beyond repair. Less than twenty-four hours earlier, my four children had been found brutally murdered. After an angry, humiliating night at the police station, George and I had been released with orders not to leave town until notified. The police had brought us here to Lan O' Lakes Motel to wait it out.

The silence was deafening. Gone were the laughter, the hugs, and all the mundane chores that come with raising children. Now the entire world seemed foreign and distant to me. I felt as if I were a tiny grain of sand encased in a fifty-five-gallon drum. I was screaming to be let out of the prison I had been unjustly thrown into, but nobody seemed to hear my cries. Nobody would let me out of the drum.

George had gone to get an evening newspaper, hoping to learn something about what had happened to the children. Finding myself alone, I cried out to God.

I knew little about this God I was crying to. I knew vaguely that He was supposed to be loving and merciful, and, as such, He couldn't possibly have wanted my children to die this way. Surely He had to be on my side.

"Please, God, H-E-A-R me!" I screamed from inside the drum. "I can't live without the kids. They're my whole life. I'm trying so hard to be strong, God, but I just can't be. Bring them back, God. Please, bring them back!"

But my words just echoed inside the drum, and I feared that not even God cared that all this was happening to me.

Suddenly a hole was punched in the drum, and a warm fluid began to fill it. The tiny grain of sand basked in the warmth. Then the drum burst open, and I was poured out into the room, a room filled with a warmth and comfort that no human language can possibly describe.

A voice answered me: *You have not lost your children. They are in My hands, and I am with you. I will give you My strength to see this through.*

It felt as if all the children were sitting on my lap. A little hand came up and wiped away my tears. I caressed the air around me, touching and holding my children. I didn't ever want to leave this corner. I had my kids back, and my heart was full again.

Slowly, peacefully, the feeling of the children faded away. I turned to search for the voice again.

You have not lost them, He repeated. *You are only separated from them for a little while. The answers you seek I will show you. It has all been written down. It has all been taken care of.*

I sat quietly for a long time, waiting for the voice to speak again. When the silence continued, I pulled the Gideon Bible from the motel desk drawer and began to read it. I knew little of the Bible, but somehow I knew that this was where it was written down. All my answers lay in these pages. I would search and I would find them.

It would take me years to find the answers, and even more years before I could apply His solution to my own life and the destiny of my children.

For years I shared my story with others and felt an odd sort of kinship as I listened to the stories of fellow victims, because only they could understand the impact of what this crime had taken from me. I traveled all over the country, speaking to audiences large and small, telling them about what had happened to my family and how Christ was returning someday soon so that I could be with my children again in the kingdom that He was preparing for us. My hope rested on the sure promise that He was coming back to take us home. This was the extent of our victory.

Everywhere I went, victims flocked to hear my story and then stayed to talk to me afterward. I realized that though we're not all victims of murder, all victims share similar insecurities and doubts and fears. Some of us have fallen prey to the most unspeakable kinds of abuse, abuse that violates us physically, mentally, and spiritually. Abuse that leaves us feeling so betrayed and worthless that we fear that not even God can fathom what we've been through.

Some of us have fallen victim to circumstances beyond our control. Nobody was ultimately to blame, but our lives are shattered nonetheless. It's hard to duck when you don't know where the bullets are coming from. It's all just so senseless. It's all so unfair.

We reach the depths of despair, and we just lie there until we finally muster the willpower to fight to our feet and claw our way back up again. We cling to the hope of His coming so that our suffering will finally be over. But we are still victims. And, without intervention, we will remain victims for the rest of our lives—

until we can grasp the full meaning of the victory that Christ won on the *other* side of the Cross.

We cannot understand the Victor until we first understand the Victim. Jesus Christ came to this earth to be a victim.

When I first realized that Christ was also a victim, I wondered if He could possibly understand the magnitude of what my children went through the night they were murdered. As I studied the scars in His hands and His feet and His side, I realized that, yes, my Savior understands. He suffered just as my children suffered. He died just as they died.

As my three-year-old daughter was being beaten over the head with the butt of a gun, a crown of thorns was being thrust on His head. As bullets ripped through my children's bodies, nails ripped through His flesh. As Tonya was being stabbed in the chest with a steak knife, Jesus was being stabbed in the side with a sword. And just as my innocent children cried out in anguish those last moments before death, so did He.

As we loved ones gathered those mangled bodies and gently laid them to rest in the earth, we could not understand how anyone could have taken those innocent lives. We cried bitter tears because we could not love them enough to save them. The Bible says that Jesus will carry the scars in His hands and His feet and His side forever, to remind us that He, too, was a victim.

But there's something unique about Jesus. While we try to avoid being victimized, He willingly came to this earth for the express purpose of being a victim. He left the glory of heaven to be betrayed, to be handed over to an angry mob, to be beaten and scourged and spat upon, to be nailed to a cross, to die an excruciating death. Yet He bore it all in silence, even showing compassion for His victimizers and those who betrayed Him.

He was King of the universe, yet He lay down all His godly powers to walk among us. He came to show us the Father. He came to teach us about salvation. But mostly, He came to die. As a man, He had no physical advantage over any of us. He suffered just as we suffer. He understands our afflictions because He was here! He loved us too much to let us suffer on this earth without hope. And He knew that the only way to give us hope was to share in our suffering.

But Jesus was not the only one who fell victim that horrible day. As I think about those who loved Him most, I realize that, like George and me, they were also victims.

The disciples watched helplessly as the Man they had believed with all their hearts to be the Promised One surrendered His last breath on that cross. All their hopes were murdered with Jesus that day. They fled in fear of their very lives. Huddled in an upper room behind a bolted door, they wept the bitter tears of grief and betrayal.

How could this have happened? They had been so sure that He was the Messiah. Now He lay in a tomb. How could everything they believed in fall apart so quickly, so violently? It was not supposed to end this way! The Man who was to be their victor ended His life as a victim instead.

If the story were to end there, we victims would have no hope. Like Him, we would remain victims, some of us in graves, others walking witnesses to the tragedies in our own lives; people covered in scars with little chance of recovery and no chance to overcome our circumstances.

But the story doesn't end there. On the third day the stone was rolled away, and Jesus Christ rose victorious from that grave. In that moment the King of the universe won the victory over death. Jesus Christ was alive!

There was no doubt of that victory when Christ revealed Himself, not just to the disciples, but also to more than five hundred people over the course of forty days. Those who saw Him alive realized they were no longer victims. It was real. Everything they had believed in was true. Jesus was the Messiah. He fulfilled the prophecies. He gave up His life on that cross, and then, with His own resurrection, conquered death itself. The kingdom He came to establish was not an earthly one as they had expected, but a heavenly one. And all who believed in Him would share in that kingdom one day soon.

It was their job now to tell the world. To tell every human being who has fallen victim to sin that the chains had been broken. The victory is ours for the asking. God's own Son was willing to come to this earth to experience *our* pain and *our* anguish, *our* death and *our* grave, and He is willing to share *His* victory with us! He didn't die on that cross for Himself. He died for us. And all we have to do is claim that victory as our own—and it's ours! We do not have to remain victims on this earth. Instead, we can stand as victors in Christ today.

Jesus didn't stay long on this earth after His resurrection. He knew He had work yet to do in heaven. The disciples watched in awe as Jesus rose into the clouds and disappeared from their sight.

But He left us with a promise. "In my Father's house are many mansions: . . . I go to prepare a place for you. And if I go and prepare a place for you, I will come again, and receive you unto myself; that where I am, there ye may be also" (John 14:2, 3, KJV).

When we read this promise, those mansions sound pretty terrific. But there's something else about the place that is even better than the mansions. Because when He comes to take us home, Jesus Christ, *the victims' Advocate,* will be our King.

And in His kingdom there will be no more death or mourning or crying or any more pain, for the former things have all passed away. (See Revelation 21:4.) For those of us who have been victims, that is an incredible promise.

Jesus came to this earth to be a victim. But He didn't remain that way. In one grand motion, He became the Ultimate Victor of the universe. It is in His victory that we, too, can be victors.

What was the difference that transformed me from a victim waiting for Christ to come, to a victor in Christ today? It was the realization that the victory is not won when He comes to takes us home. It was won the moment He came out of the tomb. If I choose to claim His victory as my own, I do not have to wait until His coming. I can be free from the chains that have held me in bondage to the past. The same Man who holds the keys to the grave and promises to take my family home, holds the key that sets me free today. "It's all been taken care of." I can have my victory now.

Once I realized that I did not have to be a victim anymore, my focus began to change. I could cling to His victory and claim it as my own. Just like the scars in Jesus' hands, my scars would remain, but they did not have to cripple me.

But since I had thought and reacted like a victim for so many years, it had become a lifestyle for me. I needed to change the way I thought about myself and how I responded to the world around me. I needed to learn to think like a victor. It was time for me to go back to the Bible. What I found there has led me on a most incredible journey.

I invite you to join me on that journey as we discover together how God can transform us from victims of the past to victors for eternity. But before we can go any farther, we must make this resolution together.

MY RESOLUTION

From this moment on, I will no longer think like a victim. I will cling to the victory that my Savior won on the other side of the Cross. It's time for me to live like a victor instead.

CHAPTER 3
ME, MYSELF, AND HIM

Keep me as the apple of your eye;
hide me in the shadow of your wings (Psalm 17:8).

When I was a kid, I felt a lot like a discarded aluminum can being kicked along the sidewalk by anybody and everybody who happened by. Sometimes I'd sit alone for days with no attention at all, but sooner or later somebody would come along. Few people seemed to be able to resist the temptation to kick this can when they saw me. I guess it could be argued that at least I was going somewhere.

Over the years I came to accept my lot in life. Obviously, I wasn't worth very much, but at least I offered some meager entertainment for those who wanted to see how far they could kick me.

But then one day something incredible happened. The most handsome man in the entire world walked by me, but instead of kicking me, he actually picked me up. He brushed the dirt off of me and said, "Why, this isn't an aluminum can at all. This is pure gold."

He's been treating me like gold for thirty-two years now. During all those years, I can honestly say that George has never intentionally done anything to hurt me. He has never hit me, cursed at me, or called me a bad name. At this point, I doubt that he ever will.

Over the years I learned that as long as I looked at myself through my husband's eyes, I had value. I was precious. I was beautiful, sexy, and talented. As long as I didn't look in a mirror or listen to anyone else, I believed every word. I did everything I could to live up to his image of me, and over the years I actually started building some self-esteem. I began to feel good about who I was.

But when someone hurt or belittled me, I took my eyes off of George and looked at myself through other people's eyes. And there I was—back on the sidewalk being kicked farther down the line. Again George would pick up what was left of me, brush off the dirt, and show me that I was gold. And I'd be OK until someone else came along and put me back on that sidewalk. My self-esteem was completely dependent upon what other people thought of me. I had no value unless others saw it in me.

In looking at myself through George's eyes, I did one thing right and one thing wrong.

I was right in not looking to myself for affirmation of my worth. Had I done so, one of two things would have happened. Either I would have concluded that I was nothing more than flesh and bone with no redeeming qualities and no real value, thus sustaining a sense of worth that equaled zero. Or I would have bolstered myself up with selfish pride, pep talks, and ego trips, thus building a very "me-centered" attitude.

I was wrong in relying on other human beings, even my loving husband, to gauge my self-worth. There will always be people in my life who wish to tear me down and others who wish to build me up. If I look to others to determine my value, my self-esteem will rise and fall according to whom I am with at the time. I will live forever on an emotional roller coaster, and I'll be constantly dizzy from trying to keep up with how much I'm worth at any given moment.

If, however, I set my gaze heavenward and look at myself through the reflection of my heavenly Father's eyes, I will have a healthy attitude and an accurate estimation of my true worth. I must never weigh my worth on other people's standards or ideals. My worth must be measured by God's scales.

We all know the song "Amazing Grace." The first line says, "Amazing grace, how sweet the sound that saved a wretch like me." We may consider ourselves wretches when we compare our glory to God's glory, but the truth is that, when God looks at us, He never sees a wretch. He sees His own precious child. He yearns for our sticky kisses and our dirty hugs. He displays our meager accomplishments on His heavenly refrigerator door for all the universe to see.

"Look at what My child made for Me." He beams at the angels. "She's so talented, isn't she? Why, she's a regular chip off the old block! She's the apple of My eye. I can't wait to spend some time with her today. I love her with all My heart."

God has so many children, and yet He has room in His heart for us all. He loves each of us individually and unconditionally.

When He looks at us, He sees the apple of His eye. (See Psalm 17:8.) He knows everything there is to know about us. Even the very hairs on our head are numbered.

The psalmist says, "O LORD, you have searched me and you know me. You know when I sit and when I rise; you perceive my thoughts from afar. You discern my going out and my lying down; you are familiar with all my ways. Before a word is on my tongue you know it completely, O LORD" (Psalm 139:1-4).

"For you created my inmost being; you knit me together in my mother's womb. I praise you because I am fearfully and wonderfully made; your works are wonderful, I know that full well" (Psalm 139:13, 14, NIV).

He knows us better than we know ourselves. God does incredible work, and we are a perfect example of it. We were made in His image! Even after the Fall in the Garden, we are described as being created a little lower than the angels, crowned with glory and honor. We are God's crowning glory in the Creation story.

But we don't feel that way when we suffer from an inferiority complex. Instead, we feel isolated, unloved, and unworthy. This low self-esteem affects our motivation both to perform and to defend ourselves against criticism. It affects our ability to cope with situations and manage our emotions. It makes us sensitive, submissive, and dependent on others. It stifles our creativity and our ability to express ourselves. It makes us insecure, withdrawn, and depressed. When people compliment us, we look right through them as if they weren't even there. The higher the praise, the less likely we are to believe it.

We don't overcome our low self-esteem by trying to bolster our own self-image with selfish pride. Rather, we need to look at ourselves the way God looks at us. Focusing on ourselves through our Father's eyes helps us to realize that we are not the center of the universe; He is. It is not all about us; it's all about Him. He is our Creator, our Sustainer, and our Salvation.

It is not our job to try to meet other people's expectations. It is not our job to place too high a standard on ourselves. Rather, we should seek to attain the standard that God has set for us.

Self-esteem is not the same as pride. Pride is haughty, arrogant, and self-centered. It looks inward for self-worth and outward for affirmation and praise from others.

One can have good self-esteem and still have humility. Humility thinks of others. It recognizes and respects the needs, gifts, and desires of others. Humility depends on God and realistically appraises oneself through His eyes.

Sin is living independent of God. Self-esteem without God invites pride. Self-esteem with God invites humility. God-based self-esteem is not superior, stubborn, or self-willed. It recognizes God's supremacy. It is God-willed.

Christians can have positive self-images, not because of anything we've done, but because of who we are in relationship to God. His grace, born of unconditional love for His children, is what makes the unworthy worthy to be heirs to His kingdom.

In Luke 15 we are told the story of the prodigal son. As the story goes, the young man went to his father and asked for his inheritance so he could enjoy it while he was still young. The father obliged the boy. Shortly after that, the young son set off for a distant country, where he squandered his wealth in wild living.

After he had spent everything, there was a severe famine in the land, and the young man began to be in need. So he hired himself out to a farmer and was sent out to the fields to feed the pigs. He longed to fill his stomach with the pods that the pigs were eating, but no one gave him anything to eat.

When he came to his senses, he said to himself, *My father feeds his servants better than this, and here I am starving to death.*

He decided to go back home. He would throw himself at his father's feet and tell him, "Father, I have sinned against heaven and against you. I am no longer worthy to be called your son; make me like one of your hired men" (vv. 18, 19).

But when he came near to his boyhood home, his father saw him and was filled with compassion for him. He ran to his son, threw his arms around him, and kissed him.

"Father," the son cried. "I have sinned against heaven and against you. I am no longer worthy to be called your son" (v. 21).

But the father ignored the son's words and called to his servants. "Quick! Bring the best robe and put it on him. Put a ring on his finger and sandals on his feet. Bring the fattened calf and kill it. Let's have a feast and celebrate. For this son of mine was dead and is alive again; he was lost and is found" (vv. 22–24).

This story brings out several important truths. First, the prodigal son had once enjoyed a respectable life as the son of a wealthy man. He knew who he was and where he came from.

But when he left home, He lost sight of whose child he was. He lost his self-esteem. Only after he hit bottom did he decide to return, not expecting to be reinstated as a son, but to be treated as a servant. He knew even his father's servants were treated with more respect and value than he himself enjoyed as a pig tender in a distant country.

But in his shame, it didn't occur to him that he might be restored to his previous status. He had blown it. He had failed. He had squandered everything. He had shamed the family name. He was no longer worthy to be called a son.

His father never even considered such a thought. This young man continued to be his precious son. Nothing the young man could ever do would change his father's feelings for him.

Every one of us belongs to God. We are His children, and He cherishes us. We can be like the prodigal son and turn our backs on our Father's love, but that doesn't change His feelings for us. God stands at the door and waits for His precious children to return to Him. When we finally get tired of battling the world and choose to go home, there is great rejoicing. There is nothing our Father yearns for more than the affection of His children.

It's time for us to quit looking at ourselves through other people's eyes and start seeing what God sees when He looks at us. It's time for us to quit judging ourselves by what we can or cannot do, what we have or have not done, or what we will or will not accomplish in the future. Our destiny is in the hands of our Creator. It's time for us to focus on who we are in relationship to our Father.

We are heirs to His kingdom. We're the reason Christ came to this earth and died on the cross. We're the reason He paid the ransom. Because, to Him, we are priceless. We are irreplaceable.

Only you can fill your place in your Father's heart. No one else will do.

MY RESOLUTION

From now on, I will not judge myself by what others think of me. I will look at myself through my Father's eyes. I am fearfully and wonderfully made. I am the apple of His eye.

CHAPTER 4
MY GOD IS BIGGER

He alone is my rock and my salvation; he is my fortress,
I will not be shaken (Psalm 62:6).

I sat at a table stacked high with books ready for me to autograph. A young woman stood at the ready to replenish the stacks as they went down. The line in front of me ran as far as I could see.

I had been invited to this camp meeting to share my story of tragedy and triumph and had spoken in the auditorium for an hour. But I knew from previous experience that my evening was far from over. Though I had spent a lot of time preparing for the previous hour, it was the time that lay before me that was the most important. It was time for me to stop talking and start listening.

Many would wait for hours just for a chance to share their own tragedy with me. I knew that those who stood along the sidelines waiting for the crowd to thin out were the ones who had endured the most. They'd ask for a hug, and as I stood to embrace them, I'd hear the words, "I lost a son, too." "My daughter was killed last year." "I was abused by my father."

Tears would flow as they shared the details of their own personal tragedies and gained comfort in knowing that somebody out there knew the depths of their pain. Long after the bookstore had closed, I would still be here, standing outside listening, sympathizing, encouraging. And somehow, I, too, would gain courage from them, knowing that I, too, was not alone in my pain.

Victims don't tell me their stories because I'm a counselor or a psychologist. They trust me with their pain because, like them, I have been a victim. We tend to seek out people to whom we can relate. We gravitate toward those who have shared our experiences, our trials, and our struggles. We read true-life stories of real people who have risen to the challenge and beat incredible odds because they give us hope that we can too.

But too often we put people on pedestals that they do not deserve. Time after time I've heard a fellow victim say, "If Joy can get through that, I can surely get through my own tragedy. Mine is nothing compared to hers."

I'm not a superhero! I don't have some secret superhuman strength to endure the things that have happened to me and to keep me from falling into a deeper hole. The truth is that there is only one depth of despair. Mine was no deeper or darker than anyone else's.

Once we reach the bottom, we have two choices. We can give up, or we can look up and start looking for a way out of that hole. That incredible will to survive does not come from us. It's there because God put it there. The fact that we can recover from life's tragedies has nothing to do with how strong we are, but how strong our God is.

The Bible is full of examples of real people just like us. They weren't superheroes any more than we are. They all were born selfish and me-centered, with insecurities and character flaws just like we have. And yet God called these ordinary people to perform very specific duties for Him. Some of those duties were immense, and the Bible contains stories of people telling God, "I don't want to do it. I can't do it. I don't have the skills and the personality needed to accomplish this task."

If none come to mind, read about Moses and Jonah and Jeremiah. All three balked at the idea of doing something great for God. All three swore they lacked the ability to do what God called them to do.

But God said, "Yes, you do. You have Me. And if you have Me, you have everything you need."

It's marvelous—God tells us all the very same thing. If we have God, we have everything we need for any situation.

But too often we forget that resource. Sometimes we start out on some task fully confident that God is with us. But somewhere in the middle, the devil trips us up and spins us around; this makes us dizzy and takes our eyes off the Savior. Suddenly we lack the confidence we need to go forward.

But we're not the first ones to lose confidence, and we're certainly not going to be the last. We can be encouraged that we're in good company. And no matter how many times we lose sight of God and flail about blindly on our own, He stands there ready to grab us before we fall.

King David is a perfect example of what I'm talking about. David was just a boy when God chose him to be the next king of Israel. God saw something in David that He could use, even though God Himself didn't want Israel to have a king at all.

Sometimes God lets us have our way even when it's not in our best interest. We need to be careful what we pray for because we just might get it. We need to be surrendered to His will in every aspect of our lives, completely confident that if we surrender to Him, He will supply all our needs.

As a boy, David had complete confidence in His heavenly Father. He believed that there was nothing that God could not do for His people. He truly exhibited the attitude "if God is with me, who can stand against me?" It was this attitude that sent him onto a battlefield with only a sling and a prayer to take down Goliath, while the entire Israelite army shrank at the prospect and watched a boy do their job.

Never once did David show any fear. He knew that God would give him this victory. This little showdown wasn't between David and Goliath. As far as David was concerned, it was between God and Goliath, and David knew that *His* God was a whole lot bigger than *their* giant.

But as David grew older, he seemed to have lost some of that confidence. He began to let his own emotions and his own desires get in the way of letting God lead in His life. Many of us today suffer from the same problem that David did.

I love to read the psalms when I'm feeling emotional. It doesn't matter what emotion I'm feeling, there's a psalm that speaks to it. Women are said to be more emotional than men. But if you read the psalms of David, you find a man whose emotions were all over the place!

One minute he's singing at the top of his lungs: "I will praise You, O Lord, with all my heart." The next moment he is so deep in the pit of despair that he can't even see the rim: "My God, my God, why have You forsaken me? I cry out by day, but You do not answer."

The next thing we know he's praising God again: "I waited patiently for the Lord; He turned to me and heard my cry. He lifted me out of the slimy pit, out of the mud and mire; He set my feet on a rock and gave me a firm place to stand. I will trust in the Lord forever." But soon we find him begging for God to hear his pleas for deliverance, wondering if God will ever answer Him: "How long, O Lord? Will You forget me forever? How long will You hide Your face from me?"

We ask ourselves, Can't this grown man get control of his emotions? He's the king of Israel! What happened to that confident young boy who crossed the battlefield with a sling in his hand and God as his shield?"

David is a perfect example of you and me. We let life get in the way of our own victories. We lose sight of God in the midst of our trials, and we write our own psalms to God, using our own emotions, every day.

You know what I mean. We sing praises to God on the way to work and then mutter choice cuss words about the driver in front of us because he didn't respond quickly enough to the green light. We go about our day just happy as a lark, so thankful to be alive, only to stub our toe on the vending machine and completely lose our self-control. And when it's time to head home after a difficult day at work and the car won't start, we ask, "Where are You, God? Why have You forsaken me? What did I do to deserve all this?"

What can we do to keep ourselves focused on God during all our trials so that we aren't tossed to and fro by our own emotions? Our answers can be found in the example of another man from the Bible. His name was Daniel.

Daniel was just a young man when he was taken captive to Babylon. Unlike David, who stood confidently before Goliath and claimed God's victory as his own, Daniel had no illusions that he might overpower his captors and run back home where he belonged. But in spite of his impossible circumstances, Daniel made a promise to himself and his God. He would remain faithful to the values he had been taught no matter what circumstances lay before him.

Time and again Daniel faced certain death, but never once did he waver. Daniel was no Samson. But he didn't depend on his own strength and power. He depended on God to supply it for him. God didn't keep Daniel *out* of captivity, but He kept hold of him *in* his captivity. God didn't prevent Daniel from being tempted by the king's food or the king's schools. But He gave him the fortitude to eat only healthful food. God didn't prevent him from being thrown into the lions' den when Daniel refused to worship the king. But He shut the lions' mouths so that no harm was done to him.

Daniel prayed to God three times a day, but he communed with Him constantly. Daniel didn't try to lean on his own strength and understanding. He never felt betrayed or abandoned or forsaken by God. In all situations he had absolute faith that God was with him and that even if he lost his life in the name of the Lord, the victory was his for the asking.

It's time for us to stop letting emotions and experiences of our past dictate how we feel about ourselves and how we react to our circumstances. It's time for us to think like Daniel. We must choose to lean on God in all situations and trust that He will be there for us and supply all our needs. As we learn to lean on Him, He will give us the fortitude we need to be transformed from victims of the past to victors for eternity.

Daniel knew the secret. He chose God. And God never let Him down. No matter what happens in our lives, God will never let us down; He is there as both our Counselor and our Comforter. And though there are thousands of us who need Him to listen and sympathize and encourage, we don't have to wait in line for hours just to gain a few moments of His time. His attention is entirely ours every moment of every day.

There is no pain so great that He cannot ease it. No suffering so horrible that He cannot give us the endurance to survive it. No loss so permanent that He cannot restore it. We can rest in the knowledge that He is here for us today. He is the superhero we seek. He is all we need to overcome our trials.

MY RESOLUTION

From this day forward, I choose God. I will not depend on my own meager ability to cope. I will lean on Him for my strength and my salvation. I will commune with Him not just daily, but moment by moment.

CHAPTER 5
THE CHOICE IS OURS

Do not conform any longer to the pattern of this world, but be transformed by the renewing of your mind. Then you will be able to test and approve what God's will is—his good, pleasing and perfect will (Romans 12:2).

I enjoy playing with words. When I started playing with the two words *victim* and *victor*, I found something that I thought was very interesting. Both words start with the same four letters. It's the last two letters that make the difference. The word *victim* ends in I M. I'm a vict**im**. I'm focused on myself alone, and I'm a victim. **Or** I can make a choice in my life. I can quit focusing on myself, make a choice, an OR, if you will, and turn myself into a vict**or** instead.

OR

Vict~~I'm~~ = Vict<u>OR</u> — Either *I'm* a vict*im*, *or* a Vict*or*.

The choice is entirely ours. Once we come to that realization and make the choice, our transformation begins. So where do we go from here? Suddenly the world looks a little different. We are no longer the conquered. We are conquerors.

But we've never thought as a conqueror before. How do we begin?

First, we have to change our attitude about those ugly scars that life has left behind. Every victim has them—and they are not all going to vanish. It's not just our flesh, but also our hearts and our minds that are scarred by the tragedies in our lives. Not all of our questions about the past are going to be answered to our satisfaction. Not every issue will be resolved. Not everything that has been taken away from us will be restored in this life. We must face the fact that some of these scars we will carry to our graves.

In the past, we have let those scars affect how we feel about who we really are and how the world looks back at us. But if we are to be victors, then those scars must no longer stand as bleak reminders of past tragedies. We need to quit viewing them as scars and begin to regard them as Purple Hearts—medals of valor earned in battle. We are survivors. Wear them proudly as Christ wears His.

Second, we need to recognize that the war is far from over. As victors, it's time to learn to fight smart. We must start by making the choice right now never to be victims again. It is our job as Christians to do everything humanly possible to avoid any situation that might set us up to be victimized, either by another human being or by circumstance.

Solomon pointed out that "the highway of the upright avoids evil; he who guards his way guards his life" (Proverbs 16:17). We are to use the good sense God gave us to keep ourselves out of obviously harmful situations. We need to choose our relationships wisely and avoid being in the company of those who may prey upon us. If someone has hurt you in the past and that person continues to hurt you, it's time to ask God for the courage to break those bonds and be set free.

This can be an incredibly scary concept. You alone know all the details of your circumstances and what your victimizer may be capable of. It will not be easy, but you are not in a hopeless situation.

Penny* remained in an abusive relationship for more than twenty years. Like other victims of abuse, she blamed herself for the way Bruce* treated her and even defended his actions to others. Somehow, she deserved to be cursed, belittled, and tormented. Besides, when Bruce's actions got really bad, he always apologized and promised that things would change. And things would change for a few weeks. But then the abuse would begin again, each time a bit worse than before.

Many times Penny thought about leaving him, but Bruce made good money, and he provided well for her and their four children. Penny was thankful that Bruce's job kept him out of town much of the time. When Bruce did come home, she and the children would do their best to stay out of his way. The children learned to curse right back at their father and to manipulate him into giving them the material things they wanted. Bruce never cared. In his eyes he had complete control of his family, and that was just the way he liked it.

As the years passed, Bruce's need to control and manipulate his family grew even more intense. Penny was terrified of him, but she was even more terrified of what might happen to her and the children if she left him. Bruce had never allowed her to work outside the home, so she had developed no marketable skills. How could she possibly provide for her children without Bruce's income?

And so Penny stayed, convincing herself that it wasn't so bad after all. It must be at least partly her fault that Bruce treated her the way he did. She prayed that Bruce would be involved in a fatal accident and longed for the day when she would finally escape the consequences of the poor choices she had made years before. She counted the years until the youngest would turn eighteen. In deep despair, she realized she would never survive that long.

Finally she gained the courage to tell Bruce that counseling was the only thing that would save their marriage. Amazingly, Bruce agreed—not to a counselor, but to a mediator, who would help them work out their differences. Penny insisted that Bruce choose the one they would see. So they began to visit with a mediator once a week.

In her entire career this mediator had never once recommended that anyone leave his or her spouse. Her experience told her that any situation could be worked out with proper counseling.

For weeks Penny confided her darkest secrets, as Bruce worked his magic to manipulate the mediator into seeing things his way. Finally the mediator asked to speak with the children in private to learn what they might say about their father's abuse. Afterward the mediator called Penny into the room.

She told Penny that hers was one of the worst cases of verbal abuse she had ever encountered. Though Bruce rarely caused any physical damage, his teasing, tormenting, taunting, and temper tantrums were all ways to control his family, and that constituted abuse. For the sake of the children, as well as for Penny, the mediator recommended that Penny and the children leave Bruce immediately. Penny took her advice.

It has been four years now since Penny had the courage to move out. Bruce is no longer Penny's husband, but because he is entitled to regular visitation rights with the children, he remains a formidable force in her life. Though Bruce is now remarried, he continues his mind games on both Penny and the children, seemingly bent on destroying them all. Sadly, his children will never have a healthy father-child relationship, and the cycle of abuse is likely to continue into the next generation. Only time will tell.

It will be many years before the youngest turns eighteen and Penny can be completely free of the bonds that have held her for more than two decades. But she's working on it. Although Bruce has not yet gotten the message, she has made the decision that she will no longer be Bruce's victim.

Penny and the children never missed a meal after she made her decision to leave. Her greatest fear of being alone and defenseless was unfounded, for God has truly provided. Her greatest struggle now is learning how to trust. But God is patient with His children. He knows just what we need to overcome our trials. He has brought a wonderful man into Penny's life who loves her unconditionally and treats her like the gold she really is.

God uses people, and He's using Scott* to teach Penny how to trust and to love without fear. Only then can she fully trust her heavenly Father to supply all her needs. Scott's influence can potentially make a positive impact on the children.

Scott and Penny are building a new life together that is centered on Christ. Their lives are far more complicated than they should have to be, but they are enduring it together. I pray for them daily and thank God for sending Scott to Penny. Scott is an illustration of God's assurance that He will never leave us nor forsake us. God is right there beside us no matter how many darts the devil throws at us. With God beside us, we can endure all things.

The Bible tells us not to fear for the future. Not to worry about what you will eat or wear. For our heavenly Father knows what we need. If we first seek His kingdom, our necessities will be provided. We don't have to worry about tomorrow. (See Matthew 6:31–34.) We have no excuse to stay in an abusive relationship when we have a heavenly Father who longs to take care of us.

If you are currently in an abusive situation, it's time to let go of all your fears and let God take care of you. Any fears that you may have are unfounded *if* you lean on God for all your needs. He promises He will never leave us nor forsake us.

Also remember that God often uses other people to help meet our needs, and He has placed people in our paths to help us. Confide honestly with a pastor or trusted friend. Find out what resources your city or state has available to help you to break away from your situation safely. Use your head, pray for guidance, and move forward. God will do the rest.

You will never again be anyone's victim.

MY RESOLUTION

If I am to live like a victor, I must do more than overcome the past. I must take whatever steps necessary to never be a victim again. I will seek God's guidance in breaking any chains that are holding me in bondage. I will set myself free.

---

*Not their real names.

CHAPTER 6
LEAVE THE WALLS BEHIND

Be strong in the Lord and in his mighty power. Put on the full armor of God so that you can take your stand against the devil's schemes (Ephesians 6:10, 11).

We all know the story of the Three Little Pigs. One was wise and two were foolish. All three built houses that provided adequate shelter against the weather. But only the wise little pig designed his house to withstand the threat of the Big Bad Wolf that lurked in the woods nearby. Neither the straw house nor the stick house were any match against the Big Bad Wolf's huffing and puffing, and the two little builders fled their ruins for the safety of their brother's little brick fortress.

As kids, we all admired that smart little pig for planning ahead. When that Big Bad Wolf came a-huffing and a-puffing, the thick brick walls didn't even budge. So the Big Bad Wolf looked for another way to penetrate the stronghold. He climbed up on the roof and started to slide down the chimney.

Just when we thought those little pigs were pork chops, the third little pig came up with another idea. He outsmarted that old wolf by lighting a fire in the fireplace and setting that wily wolf's tail a-smoldering. The Big Bad Wolf jumped out of the chimney and headed for the hills, and the three little pigs lived happily ever after in their little brick fortress at the edge of the woods.

It seems like such a nice ending to the story, but really it's not. There's no way that the three little pigs lived happily ever after, because they knew that wolf was still out there. They knew he'd be back looking for a way to catch them off guard so he could devour them. Those little pigs never ventured more than a few feet from that little brick fortress because it was the only place of safety they had. Outside those thick brick walls, they were completely vulnerable.

After we lost the children, George and I acted much like those three little pigs. We built our own little brick fortress to protect ourselves from further losses. We had three more children whom we raised inside our little brick fortress. We homeschooled them to keep them safe with us and very rarely let anyone else inside.

We did manage to put wheels under our fortress, and we traveled in it to church and town. In fact, we brought it right into church with us, parked it in the last pew, and watched the sermon from the security of our own little brick stronghold. Our children grew up and left the fortress to face the world on their own, leaving George and me alone in the fortress once more.

About a year after our youngest turned eighteen and moved out, something incredible began to happen. George and I started stepping out of the fortress and actually daring to interact with others. Over time, we began to spend more time outside the fortress, feeling incredibly vulnerable at first and selecting only "safe times" to venture out, allowing church members to show that they truly loved us.

During that year we learned to depend on the safety of our own fortress less and less. We began to crave healthy relationships with other people and even accepted invitations to their homes. We actually began to trust people outside our immediate family! One day we made the decision to abandon our fortress altogether. After twenty years, we no longer needed it.

It wasn't because the Big Bad Wolf as we perceived him was no longer lurking out there. We knew he was still out there just as big as you please. The reason we finally were able to leave our brick walls behind us was that we found an even better way to protect ourselves from danger. We discovered an incredible protective system that allowed us to move about freely so we could interact with other people and build healthy relationships. It was something the three little pigs never found.

George and I are not the first victims who have protected themselves from further hurt by building their own brick fortresses. As victims, we become master wall builders, and we can pack some mighty strong mortar between our thick brick walls. In fact, we can build our walls so high and so thick that almost nobody can penetrate our self-built fortresses. We rarely open the door to let anybody in because we're afraid that even the innocent looking little pigs may be wolves in pigs' clothing.

Many of us are also aware that, while human beings can be formidable foes, there is a force far greater than that at work against us.

The Bible says, "Our struggle is not against flesh and blood, but against the rulers, against the authorities, against the powers of this dark world and against the spiritual forces of evil in the heavenly realms" (Ephesians 6:12). We are not battling against mere humans; we're fighting against forces we don't even see!

Peter tells us to "be self-controlled and alert. Your enemy the devil prowls around like a roaring lion looking for someone to devour" (1 Peter 5:8).

Satan does more than just huff and puff and climb down chimneys. He'll do anything in his power to try to destroy us.

He's had six thousand years of practice, and he's perfected many techniques. He still uses the same tactics he used on Adam and Eve, and they still work because people forget to depend on God.

Instead, we depend on our own meager ability to protect ourselves. We lock ourselves into our own self-built fortresses. In doing so, we isolate ourselves from the rest of the world. We deny ourselves the opportunity to love and laugh and trust in healthy relationships. As long as we stay in our fortress, living happily ever after can never happen for us.

What George and I discovered after twenty years in our own fortress was that God offers us a different kind of protection, a suit of armor that protects us from injury yet allows us to move about freely in the world, to interact with people and join ourselves with others in healthy relationships.

Ephesians tells us to "be strong in the Lord and in his mighty power. Put on the full armor of God so that you can take your stand against the devil's schemes" (6:10, 11).

God doesn't urge us to arm ourselves. He doesn't advise us to be strong in and of ourselves. Instead, He invites us to use His strength, to depend on His power, to shield ourselves with His armor in order to be victorious. To me, that's an incredible invitation. And it sounds so easy, and yet it is so hard for victims to gain the courage to come out of our own fortresses and trust in God's ability to protect us with His armor.

So, what is this armor? you ask. Can it really protect me?

I assure you, God doesn't send us out to battle in our underwear. He provides us with the full ensemble! He tells us to put on the belt of truth, the breastplate of righteousness, the shield of faith, the helmet of salvation, and the sword of the Spirit. (See Ephesians 6:14–17.)

And don't forget to pin those Purple Heart medals right on the front of that breastplate. Don't they look fine on such a dazzling armor? Wear them with pride, because they tell others, "I've been through battle, and I've been wounded. I was down, but I didn't stay down."

It makes even the devil think twice about attacking you now, because he knows whose army you are fighting with.

Once we've put on all of that armor, there's one more thing God asks us to do. Pray! Pray on all occasions with all kinds of prayers and requests. (See Ephesians 6:18.)

God not only fits us for battle, but then He gives us the courage and the wisdom to stand victorious with Him. He's right there fighting alongside us, even jumping in front of us when necessary to take the sword Himself. That's what He did on the cross. He jumped in front of us. He died for us. And then He rose again!

That is why we can wear the helmet of salvation, because salvation is truly ours! It protects our heads from fatal injury. The devil is no match for it. Even if he succeeds in killing our mortal bodies, he has no power over our salvation. Our victory has already been won.

Jesus demonstrated how effectively the belt of truth worked when He was tempted by the devil in the wilderness. Satan used Scripture to try to trip up Jesus, but Jesus knew the Scriptures too. Even more than that, Jesus had a healthy relationship with His Father. He knew the truth, and the truth was His defense against Lucifer's deception. Deuteronomy 20:4 tells us that " 'the LORD your God is He who goes with you, to fight for you against your enemies, to save you' " (NKJV).

God provides all the protection we need to stand against the devil's schemes. He is the difference between our being victims locked in our own fortress prisons and being victors in *any* situation.

The shield of faith is probably the most important part of God's ensemble. Enemy arrows just bounce right off of it, and it's big enough to protect the entire body. There isn't a weapon Satan can invent that will penetrate it. And it protects front and back at the same time! There's no way to get around it.

While the shield of faith is protecting us, God gives us the sword of the Spirit to actually get in a few licks of our own. The Spirit is the ultimate weapon of destruction against the evil one because it is so multifunctional. The Spirit offers us all the strength, courage, wisdom, and endurance we need for the battle we face. And if the Spirit lives in us, nobody can knock that sword out of our hands.

It's time for us to make the decision to come out of our own self-built fortresses and put on the full armor of God. It's time for us to quit isolating ourselves from the rest of the world and to quit living in fear.

Remember the story of the Bubble Boy who was born with no immune system? His parents modified two rooms in their home to create a germ-free fortress for their son. They couldn't even touch him except through gloves attached to the clear plastic walls that separated him from his family.

Finally a protective bubble suit was created for the boy. I remember watching the movie based on his life and feeling both his anxiety and his excitement as he stepped out into the world for the first time. Though the suit was restrictive and cumbersome, the boy reveled in his newfound freedom, still protected in his germ-free environment. At last, he was free!

God's armor protects us from anything in life that may try to harm us, but unlike the bubble suit, it isn't restrictive or cumbersome to wear. It's made of an incredible space-age material that is so light that we don't even feel it. God's armor doesn't hinder us in any way. Instead, it sets us free!

There is one limitation about God's armor, however. It's designed for defense, not offense. It is given to us so that we can take our stand against the devil's schemes, so that we can stand strong to the end. It's designed to protect us. It's not meant to be used in seeking revenge against those who have hurt us.

I know you've been hurt. I have too. But the Bible tells us, "Never pay back evil for evil to anyone. Respect what is right in the sight of all men. If possible, so far as it depends on you, be at peace with all men. Never take your own revenge, beloved, but leave room for the wrath of God, for it is written, 'Vengeance is mine, I will repay,' says the Lord" (Romans 12:17–19, NASB).

If we take God at His word, He will repay the evil that has been done against us. But we must never forget that our God is first and foremost a God of justice and love. He admonishes us, "Do not be overcome by evil, but overcome evil with good" (Romans 12:21, NASB).

We'll discuss revenge in a later chapter. We have other issues to deal with first. The chapters that follow will help you to think outside the box and look at life in a broader sense. When we learn to do that, we are able to look at vengeance in a different way. So stick with me. Step outside those brick walls. Tighten that belt of truth another notch. Your training has just begun.

MY RESOLUTION

I will come out of my own self-built fortress and put on the full armor of God. This will allow me to move about freely and form healthy relationships with others. I will wear my scars as Purple Hearts, proud that I am a survivor.

CHAPTER 7
THIS IS ONLY A TEST

Consider it pure joy, my brothers, whenever you face trials of many kinds, because you know that the testing of your faith develops perseverance. Perseverance must finish its work so that you may be mature and complete, not lacking anything (James 1:2–4).

Wearing a full set of armor certainly changes the way you look at the world, doesn't it? Don't you feel a whole lot more secure with all that protection? It does a lot for your confidence too. Just remember that both the armor and the attitude are given to you by God. You're His soldier now. It's time to start practicing some defensive moves in that new uniform. Let's see what we can do to break in that suit a little bit. While we're at it, let's see about breaking in the new attitude that comes with it.

This new suit of clothes does not give you license to run out onto the battlefield picking fights for the fun of it. You're not an eight-year-old boy with a new pair of karate pajamas kicking Mama's flowerpots off the porch. This suit of armor is more for defense than for offense. Even more than that, like karate, it's less about defense than about discipline. Without discipline we can really get ourselves into trouble. We are not assigned to start battles—with either humans or devils. But God certainly gives us both permission and power to resist them. David didn't start the fight with Goliath, but he sure ended it.

When my son, Cody, was fourteen, he talked constantly about wanting a dune buggy so he could go up into the mountains and play. He seemed quite emphatic about one feature that he had to have—a roll bar. One day I asked him why a roll bar was so important to him.

"Because I want to be able to roll the dune buggy for fun," he answered.

"Cody," I laughed, "a dune buggy is designed to handle rough terrain. The roll bar isn't there *so* you can roll it. It's there to protect you *if* you do."

Needless to say, Cody never got a dune buggy, because I knew his attitude wasn't right and it wouldn't be safe for him to have one. He would abuse the privilege and get himself hurt.

God acts on our behalf just as any good parent would. If we're going to misuse the armor only to hurt others or ourselves, God will take it away from us, and we will stand defenseless on the field. If we think we're so tough, God will let us prove ourselves otherwise.

In some senses, God's armor is a lot like that dune buggy. Here on earth we're in rough terrain. But instead of dreading the journey and worrying about getting stuck in the middle of nowhere, God furnishes us with a way to meet the challenge and even have a little fun along the way. But let's not forget to be on our toes. It's still dangerous out there. We could still find ourselves in a real emergency. How we handle that emergency is strictly up to us. Fortunately, life gives us plenty of opportunities to practice.

When I was in school, we had fire drills to prepare us for a real emergency. When we heard that alarm go off, our job was to remain calm, look to our teacher to give us additional instructions, and leave the building through the nearest exit—single file, no pushing. Once outside, we were to meet at the edge of the playground for a head count. When the emergency was declared over, we filed back into the building the same way we came out—single file, no pushing—and classes resumed.

Everyday life is filled with opportunities for us to drill ourselves, to help us prepare for the real emergencies in our lives. I'm not suggesting that we spend all our sunny days braced against tragedy, jumping at every sound, expecting something bad to happen. But we can use minor inconveniences and small tragedies to practice putting things in their proper perspective so that we can stand strong when the big ones come at us.

We have to remember to stay calm, to look to our Teacher for instructions, and trust that He will lead us safely through the situation. When the situation subsides, we can go back to our normal routines.

It's all about attitude. The armor allows us to move about freely instead of locking ourselves into our own protective shells for fear of what's out there. But it's our attitudes about what is happening around us and how we react to those happenings that count. We've got to learn to stand strong and roll with the punches.

When someone slams a grocery cart into your car, that's a fire drill. When your neighbor starts mowing his lawn just after you lay down for a nap, that's a fire drill. When one of the kids spills grape juice on the brand-new carpet, that's a fire drill. When your best friend criticizes what you're wearing and you thought you looked really good in the outfit, that's a fire drill. When your mom tells you to take out the trash, do the dishes, and clean your room when you've got a mountain of homework that's due the next day, that's a fire drill.

Instead of dreading the irritating and aggravating things that happen to us all, start looking at them as opportunities to practice. Pray before reacting to any situation. Ask God how to handle each circumstance. Look at yourself through your Father's eyes and conduct yourself in a manner befitting a child of the King. Practice truly does make perfect.

Joseph was a master of the fire drill. He used every circumstance that he encountered as practice to strengthen His faith in God. Though he was sold as a slave when he was only a teenager, he didn't allow his circumstances to get the best of him. In his youth he had worn with pride the coat of many colors that his father had given to him. But it was the suit of armor provided by his heavenly Father that he prized the most. He went into Egypt wearing every piece of that armor, and he learned how to use it to its fullest advantage. God's armor gave Joseph the courage to stand for the right no matter what happened to him.

Joseph did not loosen the belt of truth when Potiphar's wife tried to seduce him and then lied to her husband about what really had happened. He stood before Potiphar wearing the breastplate of righteousness, knowing that even if Potiphar would not believe him, in his heart, integrity reigned. He knew that the penalty for such a crime was death, but he also knew that even if he should die, God's helmet assured his salvation. When he was thrown into prison, he rested in the knowledge that the shield of faith had spared him. Seven years later it was the sword of the Spirit that would release him and so impress Pharaoh as to place him as governor over all of Egypt.

Joseph could have caved in during any of these circumstances. But he wore the armor instead. He used every situation in his life as a captive to reflect God's character. He knew which side of the battle he was fighting on, and he fought valiantly. Think of the kind of witness Joseph was to all those unbelieving people. What kind of a difference did Joseph make in so many lives by practicing his faith in every circumstance? Could he have made that kind of difference if he had built his own walls of defense and depended on his own strength and understanding? Could he have even survived?

What about your life? What kind of example will you be? The alarm has gone off. The drill has begun. What does our Teacher instruct us to do?

Don't panic. Don't run. Don't trample others in your effort to flee the scene. Pay attention. Think clearly. Be civil. Come out of the situation with your life and your dignity intact.

Everyday life is just a fire drill. It's an opportunity for us to grow. It's a chance for us to learn to use God's armor and land on our feet every time. As we learn to roll with the punches in everyday life, we will roll with the punches in the real tragedies as well.

MY RESOLUTION

From this moment forward, I will look at every situation as practice for the big things. I will use God's armor to my fullest advantage. Like Joseph, I will behave with integrity in all situations.

CHAPTER 8
RISE TO THE CHALLENGE

I can do everything through him who gives me strength
(Philippians 4:13).

To me, Harland Samuels is a hero, not so much because of what he did while he was serving his country in Vietnam, but for what he made of himself after he came home.

I didn't know the young Harland Samuels who went off to war, a strapping 6' 3" gentle giant of a man with a passion for the outdoors and living life to its fullest. I met him many years later— many years after the trauma, the physical therapy, and the rehab that followed his return to the United States.

Physically, Harland Samuels came home only half the man that he was before. The rocket had come in so quickly that there was no time to escape it. It landed at his feet, blowing off both of his legs and half of his left hand.

For Harland, the real battle began after he was pulled from the battlefield, as he came face to face with the reality of life without legs. The physical therapy was torture enough, but it was the mental therapy that would ultimately determine the size of the man that would come out of this horrendous ordeal. For months Harland endured indescribable pain in his legs, even though his legs were no longer there. He fought against severe depression as he contemplated living the rest of his life in a wheel-chair.

He credits his incredible recovery to the doctors and nurses who fought alongside him in the rehab ward of a hospital in Denver, Colorado. They understood the battle he was fighting and helped Harland learn to fight in a new way. Though this battle would rage on far longer than the one he fought on that distant shore, Harland somehow regained the resolve he needed to continue to fight. There were times when he thought it would be easier simply to give up the fight, but he refused to let the reality of his circumstances defeat him. Mentally, Harland Samuels was still 6' 3" tall.

I met Harland in Eagle Rock, Missouri, where he lived with his wife, Amanda, and their youngest son. The loss of his legs seemed to have little impact on Harland's enjoyment of the out-doors. He enjoyed driving along trails in his modified Jeep. He enjoyed both deer and turkey hunting on his ATV. He rode horses on his forty acres of Ozarks hill country. He also enjoyed tubing and whitewater canoeing. He even went skiing once a year in Colorado. Rather, his wife went skiing. Harland went snowboarding.

Each of these activities came with certain risks, but Harland looked at every one of them not as risks, but as challenges to be met with enthusiasm.

On a canoe trip down the White River in Missouri, Harland and Amanda were plunged into the rapids when their canoe tipped over. Although he was wearing a life jacket, Harland found himself being flipped "head over butt" like a potato rolling down a hill. With no legs, he had no ballast to keep his head afloat. Finally Amanda caught up with him and grabbed him around the chest, giving him the ballast he needed to keep his head above the foam. Harland laughed all the way to shore.

On a hunting trip a few years back, Harland jumped off of his ATV to clear a path in the trail. As he "walked" using only his arms, his gun accidentally fired and blew off two more of his fingers.

Later, in the hospital, he told a friend, "Buck, I'm just going to blow myself away a piece at a time."

It's that sense of humor that has kept him going.

As he watched my infant son crawl along his driveway on his bare knees, Harland exclaimed, "Man, that hurts *my* knees—and I don't even have any!"

While neighbors joined in to help him build a horse barn, Harland jumped out of his wheelchair and pounded posts, drove nails, and cut boards on his table saw. But when it came time to do the roof, he climbed back into his chair and said, "I think I'll leave the roof to you guys."

For those of us who have been victims, Harland Samuels stands as an inspiration to us all. He could have looked at his physical condition and decided to become half a man. By his own attitude, he could have let one tragic incident in his life destroy him forever. But Harland chose to rise above it. He has refused to let the tragedies of the past determine his future. He does not look at himself as a victim.

In the deepest sense of the word, Harland Samuels is a victor, and the scars he carries are truly worn as Purple Hearts. He did not earn them on the battlefield in Vietnam. He earned them right here at home as he struggled to regain his life and carry on. It's what he did after the war that really counts.

We have a choice in how we will react in any situation. If we are to be victors, we, too, must be willing to look at *everything* in life as challenges to be met with enthusiasm. We can share the apostle Paul's motto: "I can do everything through him who gives me strength" (Philippians 4:13).

When we do that, problems become challenges. Circumstances become challenges. Encounters become challenges. If we are willing to look at all things as challenges, then nothing in life can defeat us.

A challenge is not a competition to be won or lost. A challenge is an opportunity to do and be the very best that we can be. Even if we do not fully succeed, a challenge well met is worthy of the effort we put into it. How we meet the little challenges of everyday life will affect our responses to the bigger challenges that we will face.

We alone make that decision. But once we choose to think positively and move forward, if we will only ask, the Holy Spirit will give us the courage, the strength, the power, the faith, and the wisdom to meet the challenge. If the Holy Spirit lives in us, all these things are at our disposal any time and anywhere. We must be willing to simply step out in faith and meet the challenge head on.

The Egyptian army was hot on their trail when the children of Israel found themselves trapped against the shores of the Red Sea. Escape seemed impossible, but God provided a way out. All it took was that first step of faith. In obedience to God's directions, Moses stretched out his hand, and the water of the Red Sea began to part, and a path appeared.

Later, when the children of Israel complained that they would all die of thirst in the desert, God again provided a way. But it took an act of faith to bring that life-giving water from the rock. Moses was told to raise his staff and tap the rock. That act of faith produced water for people and animals.

Only as we choose to step forward in faith will God grant us the power to be overcomers. Without that first step of faith, we will stand alone in our weakness and be conquered by our own doubts. And the devil stands at the ready to trip us at every corner. Part of the challenge is to quit listening to him and start listening to the Holy Spirit.

A passage in Hebrews encourages us to "lay aside every encumbrance and the sin which so easily entangles us, and let us run with endurance the race that is set before us, fixing our eyes on Jesus, the author and perfecter of faith, who for the joy set before Him endured the cross, despising the shame, and has sat down at the right hand of the throne of God" (Hebrews 12:1, 2, NASB).

The race will not always be easy, but what lies on the other side of the finish line is well worth every effort we put into getting there. Christ endured because He knew what lay on the other side of the Cross. We, too, must learn to look beyond this life and fix our gaze on the kingdom that lies just beyond our horizon. If we look at our circumstances in light of eternity, we will see that everything that we are now enduring has an end and a resolution. No damage that has been done to us on this earth is permanent. Christ is coming to restore all that we have lost. We need to fix our eyes on the prize. Then we can run the race, and run it with passion.

We are confronted with challenges every day of our lives. God uses these challenges as opportunities to develop our characters. When we try to rely only on ourselves, we pass up the opportunity to strengthen our reliance on God.

This past summer my husband went to Bozeman, Montana, to spend time with our two grown sons, leaving me to pull double duty at home. While he was gone, I went to a yard sale and got a screaming deal on a clean, used lawn mower. I was not able to try it out before buying it because it had been properly winterized, and the gas and oil had been completely drained. Since this sale was being conducted to raise funds to send Pathfinders to a national camporee, I decided to take the risk and purchase the mower anyway. Even if it didn't run, I had at least donated to a good cause.

Several days later, I filled the mower with gas and oil, reconnected the spark plug wire, primed the little primer bulb, and pulled the starter cord. Nothing happened. I pulled again . . . and again. I primed the little primer bulb, and I pulled the cord again. Sixty times I pulled at the starter cord, but the mower did not start.

Amazingly, I did not get frustrated or angry. During the entire time that George had been out of town, I had determined to lean on God as my faithful husband and provider. Over the past several days, He had answered my smallest prayers with assurance that He was there for me.

I looked up and saw my neighbor's truck rounding the corner.

Ah, I thought to myself, *if my neighbor sees me struggling to start this thing, he'll stop and help me.*

I waited until he was in sight of my yard and began to pull the starter cord ten times in succession. The mower did not start, and my neighbor drove past without stopping to help.

Now I was feeling just a little bit alone and defeated. My own efforts had been unfruitful. I knew that God often uses people to help us in times of trouble, but my neighbor had not come to my rescue. Then it occurred to me that, though I had invited God to join me as I cut the grass, I had not yet asked Him personally to start this lawn mower for me.

I leaned on the mower, bowed my head, and prayed. "Heavenly Father, I'm sorry I didn't ask for Your help first. Thank You for being right here with me. I don't know why this lawn mower isn't starting. I've given it my best effort, and it hasn't been enough. Father, You know what's wrong with it. You know I need to get this grass cut before the landlord comes knocking at the door to tell me my yard is turning into a jungle. So I'm asking You to take a look at this machine. Fix whatever needs fixing and start it for me. Thank You, Father, for caring about all the little things in my life. In Jesus' name. Amen."

I opened my eyes, paused for a moment to give God a chance to take a look at the engine, and then reached down and pulled the starter cord. The mower roared to life. I set the choke at full throttle and headed out into the jungle. The mower ran like a champ until the grass catcher was full. After I had emptied the bag, I returned to the mower.

"OK, God. Here we go again," I said.

I pulled the cord, and again the mower roared to life. For the rest of the day, that mower started on the very first pull.

God uses every opportunity to teach us to rely on Him. Sometimes He gives us the power to accomplish great things. Sometimes He puts others in our path to give us the boost we need. And sometimes He just does it Himself and shows us that ultimately He has the power to do even the impossible.

Never pass up the opportunity to see God's power at work in your life. Don't blow the opportunity by letting self run the show. Self is guaranteed to botch it up good. Vow, instead, to partner up with a Winner and watch your challenges become victories.

In every circumstance, we can simply ask ourselves, "What can God and I do together to stand victorious in this situation?

How can I use this situation as an opportunity to depend on God and to develop my character so that I can become more Christlike?"

Becoming Christlike is the work of a lifetime. It is our goal, the mark we strive toward, until the day Jesus comes to take us home.

One sentence has helped me to look at my circumstances more positively and helped me to rise to the challenges of everyday life. Whenever something happens to me that threatens to affect me in a negative way, I put it into perspective by saying, "I hope this is the worst thing that happens to me today."

No day will be as dark as the night we lost the kids. Stephanie's cancer diagnosis and death twenty days after the murders comes at a very close second. But no event since then can compare with these tragedies in my life. Compared to them, everything else is just spilled milk. And that's a good attitude because if we see every bad happening in our lives as just spilled milk, we are going to cope with it a lot better. If you've been a parent, you've cleaned up a lot of spilled milk, and you know that if you get to it right away, it doesn't stink so bad in the end.

One thing we must realize is that some things in our lives are in our power to change. Sometimes we find ourselves meeting daily challenges that we simply don't have to keep on meeting. If you don't like your job, you can do something about it. You can rise to the challenge and seek a higher goal for your life. If you need further education, rise to the challenge and find a way to get it. If doing what you like to do means making less money, then meet the challenge of simplifying your life so that you can meet your needs and enjoy the way you earn your livelihood. Don't settle for what you can get. Seek an occupation that will give your life purpose and then build your life around it.

The same holds true for where we live, what we do for entertainment, the friends we choose, and even the people we live with. Sometimes the bigger challenge is changing our circumstances instead of living with them.

How will you meet the challenges in your life?

MY RESOLUTION

From this day forward I will rise to every challenge and meet it head on. I will put my whole heart into it. I can do all things through Christ who gives me strength!

CHAPTER 9
BELIEVE GOD WILL DO WHAT HE SAYS

Have you not heard?
The LORD is the everlasting God, the Creator of the ends of the earth.
He will not grow tired or weary,
and his understanding no one can fathom.
He gives strength to the weary and increases the power of the weak.
Even youths grow tired and weary, and young men stumble and fall;
but those who hope in the LORD will renew their strength.
They will soar on wings like eagles; they will run and not grow weary, they
will walk and not be faint (Isaiah 40:28–31).

I have discovered over the years that people have many defini-
tions for the word *faith.* I used to get bogged down by well-
intentioned people who tried to expand too deeply upon the
meaning of *faith.* Finally someone gave me a definition that I can
grasp, a definition so easy that even a child can understand it.

Faith is simply believing that God will do what He says He
will do.

Whether blessings or plagues, if God says He will do it, we
can be sure that it will be done. When God told Noah He would
flood the earth, yet save his household in a boat made of His own
design, it happened just as God promised it would. Isaac was
promised to Abraham and Sarah even in their old age, and it
happened just that way. Moses was sent to tell Pharaoh about ten
plagues that would fall upon Egypt, and all ten fell just as God
commanded them. God said He would send His Son to ensure

our salvation, and that is exactly what He did. Every promise that God has made has been fulfilled—except for one, which still looms in the future. Only He knows the time and the day, but very soon, God will send His Son back to earth to bring us home.

Faith is simply believing that God will do what He says He will do. The Bible gives us hundreds of reasons to believe our God is true to His word.

The problem we have with faith is not based on God's record. It's often based on our previous experiences with other people. You see, faith and trust are closely connected. One cannot have faith in something one cannot trust. Most of us who have been victims have serious trust issues, and, unfortunately, our circumstances justify our lack of trust. There have been people in our lives who have not been trustworthy, and too often they are the very people in our lives whom we should have been able to trust: parents, spouses, loved ones, friends.

A healthy child has no qualms about jumping into her father's arms. She knows that her father will catch her. But a child who has been abused by her own father cannot possibly muster the trust it takes to jump into her father's arms. She knows that he may catch her, or he may not. She isn't willing to take the risk. She's been hurt too many times before. For her, it is safer not to trust than to take the chance and be hurt again.

The sad reality is we're more likely to be victimized by someone we know than by a stranger. That's why George and I were questioned as suspects the night our children were murdered. Previous cases have proven that the perpetrator will likely be someone the victim knew. In our case, the perpetrator was our twelve-year-old son's "best friend."

We homeschooled our three children that were born after the tragedy for several reasons. But one of those reasons was that we didn't want our children going to school and making friends with killers. We didn't even trust children!

If we can't trust people, then what can we trust?

The Bible tells us to "trust in the LORD with all your heart and lean not on your own understanding; in all your ways acknowledge him, and he will make your paths straight" (Proverbs 3:5, 6).

He's the only One who can straighten us out on this point. If we lean on our own understanding based on what we've been through, our victimized concepts of words such as *father, friend,* and *family* can affect how we perceive God. If we have had an unhealthy or abusive relationship with someone in those roles, we can't picture a healthy relationship with God as our Father or Jesus as our Friend or of all of us as part of the family of God. All we know is dysfunction and distrust.

To break that cycle, we must seek to understand healthy relationships so that we can love and trust God in a healthy way. That's why it's so important for us to come out of our fortresses and trust God's armor so we can move about freely and interact with people. If we lock ourselves in our fortresses and view life through the lens of our bad experiences, we'll never know what a healthy relationship looks like.

We may not have had a healthy relationship with our earthly father, but we can look at other people and see what a healthy relationship looks like. We can use other people as examples. This is vital, because faith is an active, healthy relationship between God and human beings. Faith that trusts, faith that loves, is faith that works.

Even if there has not been one trustworthy person in our lives, there is One in all the universe whom we can trust completely. When God says He will do something, we can be sure that He will.

God knows that we live in a world of pain and broken promises. That's why He sends us out with His armor to protect us from the world and from the prince of darkness, who governs the minds of sinful human beings.

The Bible makes it very clear. The adversary who accuses us day and night is out to destroy us. He will do whatever it takes to block our view of the Savior. He will use the most drastic means imaginable to make us believe that God is not there. But if we believe the Bible and if we have faith that God will do what He promises, then Satan has no control over us.

We have to make the decision in every situation to trust in God. He has more courage, more strength, more common sense, and more problem-solving skills than any of us could ever even begin to muster ourselves. We can put the greatest minds together in one room, we can call together the mightiest men the world knows today—and they cannot hold a candle to what God can do in the wink of an eye. Our God is an awesome God! Nothing can defeat Him.

It's when we try to cope with life all by ourselves that we get in over our heads. It's when we try to stand in our own wisdom and our own human strength that life defeats us. Life is too big for us to conquer all by ourselves. But we don't have to, and God doesn't expect us to fight it alone.

The psalmist describes God's trustworthiness: "The LORD is a refuge for the oppressed, a stronghold in times of trouble. Those who know your name will trust in you, for you, LORD, have never forsaken those who seek you" (Psalm 9:9, 10).

The Bible has many names for God. Wonderful, Eternal, Almighty, the Alpha and the Omega, the First and the Last, Redeemer, Messiah, Savior, Promised One, Rock of Ages, Bread of Life, Living Water, King of kings, Lord of lords, Prince of Peace,

Creator, Defender, Advocate, Physician, Counselor, Comforter, Father, Teacher, Master, and Friend. How can we possibly look upon His names and not trust Him? He alone can be trusted no matter what our circumstances.

The apostle Paul expressed God's faithfulness this way: "Who shall separate us from the love of Christ? Shall trouble or hardship or persecution or famine or nakedness or danger or sword? . . . No, in all these things we are *more than conquerors* through him who loved us. For I am convinced that neither death nor life, neither angels nor demons, . . . neither height nor depth, nor anything else in all creation, will be able to separate us from the love of God that is in Christ Jesus our Lord" (Romans 8:35, 37–39, emphasis added).

The situations included in these verses pretty much cover the possibilities. If none of the things listed can separate us from God, then nothing else will either. And yet, He never feels overwhelmed or inconvenienced by us. In fact, we honor God when we call on Him: "Call upon me in the day of trouble," He invites. "I will deliver you, and you will honor me" (Psalm 50:15).

Faith is believing that God will do what He says He will do. But with that faith comes action.

For centuries there has been a debate over whether we are saved by faith or by our own works. Is it our faith in God alone that assures our salvation? Or is it what we do for others in the name of Jesus that puts our name on the roster of the eternally saved? I believe that it is neither faith nor works that saves us. Rather, it is faith *that* works that assures our salvation.

A passage in James makes it very clear. "What good is it, my brothers, if a man claims to have faith but has no deeds? Can such faith save him? Suppose a brother or sister is without clothes and daily food. If one of you says to him, 'Go, I wish you well;

keep warm and well fed,' but does nothing about his physical needs, what good is it? In the same way, faith by itself, if it is not accompanied by action, is dead" (James 2:14–17; see also verses 18–24). Faith that is based on relationship is faith that works!

We don't serve God because He performs miracles for us on a daily basis. We don't worship Him because He makes our lives easy and blesses us with only wonderful things. We don't praise Him because He showers us with worldly goods.

We love God because He loves us. We love God because He will never leave us nor forsake us. He will come to us in times of trouble. "We say with confidence, 'The Lord is my helper; I will not be afraid. What can man do to me?' " (Hebrews 13:6).

If we stand in a right relationship with Him, then nothing can defeat us.

We need to delve deeper into a couple of issues relating to victims and trust. Many of us who have been victimized cannot seem to paint a healthy picture of God as a heavenly Father or Jesus as a Friend we can depend on because of past abuse inflicted by one in that human role in our lives. I have personally experienced negative responses to both of the titles Father and Friend, and I have had to work hard to overcome these negative associations.

As a child, I never really had a best friend with whom I could share my secrets and my joys. I spent my recesses alone on the swings and watched as the popular girls played four square and tetherball. Two so-called friends actually invited me to walk downtown with them one hot summer day, only to ditch me once we got there. But my own childhood memories pale in comparison to what my twelve-year-old son's best friend did to him.

On the night of the murders, Billy Dyer took off his shirt and told Greg to put it in his mouth. When Greg asked why, Billy told him, "Because I'm going to shoot you, and I don't want you to scream."

Greg became alarmed and fled around the corner of the house, but Billy called him back saying, "I was only kidding."

Greg cautiously turned the corner and returned to his friend. "It's not funny," he told Billy. "You shouldn't kid like that."

Billy pulled a .22 pistol from his waistband, aimed it at Greg, and shot him in the left eye. Greg crumbled to the ground, his last gaze falling on Billy as if to ask, "Why?" Billy then ran into the house and murdered the other three.

The Bible tells us that a friend is someone who will lay down his life for someone else. For our family, the life that Billy lay down was not his own. Billy admits that he had no motive for the killings. We had done nothing to provoke him.

For years after that, George and I trusted nobody. We taught our three new children to rely on our family alone. Their contact with peers was limited to 4-H and church activities where George and I could be there and regulate every interaction. We were together all the time. We became our children's peers.

We taught them that there is always someone out there willing to get you into trouble, but once you're caught, they will abandon you. Family could be trusted; friends could not. Our children believed every word we told them, and they stepped into the world with great caution.

How can we possibly understand the Friend we have in Jesus if we have not experienced a human friend to whom we could trust our hearts? For years George and I struggled with this issue. We kept ourselves hidden safely behind our own brick walls and allowed nobody outside our family to penetrate our fortress.

But a few years ago, George and I allowed ourselves to peek out of our fortress and look around at the people who attended our church. We watched for some time from behind the wall and even dared to step out on the porch and shake hands once a week in the lobby before services began. But we'd always go scurrying back in to listen to the sermon in the safety of our fortress.

Gradually we found ourselves cutting little windows into our fortress walls so we could have a better view of these people surrounding us. To our surprise, these people seemed to be displaying a genuine love, caring, and concern for us. We began to step out of our fortress for longer periods of time as we interacted with these people during church services and study hour and fellowship dinners.

It wasn't long before we had joined a small group of believers who met in the home of a wonderful family. It was in this small setting that we learned to step completely out of our fortress and walk around with others. We actually made friends with people! We enjoyed their company. We began to share our hope for the future, the pain of our past, and the journey toward healing.

Our progress did not go unnoticed. Church members were amazed at the transformation we had made. Surely such progress should be acknowledged, they decided. In an incredible display of love, the members of our church took up a collection, and during the children's story in the middle of the service, our pastor presented us with a tiny six-week-old miniature dachshund puppy. This was a pet we had really wanted but couldn't afford to buy for ourselves.

Without even hesitating, George named the puppy Daisy to commemorate something very special to him. He had always picked daisies for our daughter, Sandy, who was born eleven months after the others were killed. For him, daisies represented a very special display of love for the only daughter he would ever get to raise.

Daisy is our empty-nest baby, and she is welcome in every church member's home. She is an incredible gift of love.

Today George and I have a network of friends that we never thought possible. We even started a small-group meeting in our own home, and after spending a year teaching at our local Christian school, I have so deeply bonded with forty kids that my heart is bursting with happiness.

Still, we have a hard time with the word *friend*. I prefer to call all of these people my family, my brothers and sisters in Christ. They're not perfect. They're just as flawed as I am. But they love and care about me, and together we look forward to a world made new where we will all live united as one. We are God's family.

God has given this support network to teach George and me how to trust. His family has become the most precious thing on earth to us. Today George and I walk about freely in the armor that God has provided for us. We are no longer locked in our fortress, and I do not miss it. We are free to move about, to explore, to experience, and to enjoy healthy relationships with others.

In a sense, God has released us from prison. Being in a relationship with God does not bind us. It frees us to enjoy life and to enjoy it abundantly. Now I look forward to prayer meetings, small-group meetings, Sabbath School and services, potlucks, school activities with "my kids," and a myriad of other get-togethers that will continue through eternity with my family in Christ.

I may never be comfortable with the word *friend*. But God has given me a family to take its place. The benefit has been twofold, for it has helped me with my concept of a heavenly Father, as well. If I have a heavenly family, a heavenly Father fits right into that picture.

When it comes to the word *father,* George's example has had the greatest impact on me. He has been a great father to our children. He never felt the need to discipline harshly. He was and still is their companion. He is a father they can trust to listen with patience and without judgment. His life has not been perfect, and he doesn't expect his kids to be either. He loves them unconditionally. Now that they are grown, they still call and just chat with Dad about everything. They even ask for advice.

His example and the stories he's told me of his own father have helped me to see the role of a father in a healthy way. But that was not my experience with my own father. When I was growing up, my dad was an alcohol-induced rageaholic. That meant that when he was drinking, he was mean.

He was a police officer for most of the years that I was a child, which meant that my dad represented the law. When he was off-duty, he apparently felt he needed a few drinks to unwind. Except it didn't unwind him. It wound him tighter, and when he broke loose, I seemed to be one of his favorite targets.

It's not that I never deserved to be punished. To be sure, I was a rebellious child, and I rebelled against him every time his punishment was too severe for the crime. Every time he threw me on the floor and sat on my chest with my arms pinned under his knees and repeatedly back-handed my face, I vowed that whatever I had been caught doing I'd go and do twelve more times just to show him that I could. I had zero respect for him as my father. I feared him. And I hated him for that fear.

Sometimes he came at me like a freight train just because I didn't respond fast enough to his commands or because he didn't like the mood I was in at the dinner table. My brother, Rick, came to my defense a few times when the attack seemed completely senseless to him. Twice Rick took the beating for me. Once he managed to execute a perfect back-flip, and Dad missed him entirely. Rick was my hero that day.

The sad thing is that I was a tomboy. I needed a father figure to take me camping and teach me how to run power tools. But my dad never did these things with me. I have no special memories of the two of us doing anything together. I just remember him coming at me and throwing me on the floor or against the wall. I liked the wall better than the floor because I could use my hands to protect my face.

The idea of having that kind of father for all eternity is not heaven to me. If I look at the example of my own father, I cannot possibly trust in a heavenly father like that. For years, even into adulthood, I had nightmares of a bad guy who tormented me. His name was always Jack—my father's name.

Fortunately for me, I can look at my husband and how he has interacted with our children and see a clear picture of what a father is supposed to be. I can transfer that image to my heavenly Father, and in so doing, I can genuinely trust in Him.

There is a happy ending to my story about my dad. When he was sixty, God finally got his attention, and my dad gave his heart to the Lord. Today my father no longer drinks or smokes or cusses or loses his temper. He's a completely changed man. I can even have a conversation with him about the Bible.

Even more incredible than that, my dad serves as a Baptist minister for a tiny church in Climax Springs, Missouri. That church stands next door to the house where our children were murdered. The Lord truly works in mysterious ways! And if He can change my father, He can do anything!

Faith is believing that God will do what He says. No problem is too big for our God. It's time for us to stop telling God how big our problems are and start telling our problems just how big our

God is! When we start doing that, we can start watching our victories multiply.

After we lost the kids, a friend gave me a plaque displaying this motto: "I shall live each day knowing that nothing could possibly happen to me today that God and I can't handle together."

I have made this my motto for living. I invite you to do the same.

MY RESOLUTION

It doesn't matter what people have done to betray me. I believe that God will do what He says He will do. From this day forward, I will live each day knowing that nothing can possibly happen to me today that God and I can't handle together.

CHAPTER 10
CHANGE YOUR DIET

Man does not live on bread alone, but on every word that comes from the mouth of God (Matthew 4:4).

"You are what you eat."

I have no idea who first uttered those words. It was probably a mother trying to urge her children to care a little more about what they put into their mouths, and the words probably fell on deaf ears. We can blame it on appetite or gluttony or just plain sin, but the bottom line is that people are all too willing to fill themselves with junk food and still expect health and fitness. 'Taint gonna happen, folks.

We cannot build a strong, healthy body by feeding it only Fruit Loops and Hershey bars. We need vitamins and minerals and fiber and all sorts of other things if we are going to reach top performance. The choice is entirely ours. Very few of us are force fed as adults.

The Bible says that our bodies are temples for the Lord. Have you looked at your body as a temple lately? Do you look in the mirror and see a vessel for Him to fill? A special structure set apart for the Lord's work?

Unfortunately, when I look in the mirror, I see a temple that has received poor maintenance over the years. It's been well fed, but it hasn't been fed well. Too much fat and not enough muscle, to be sure, and I am ashamed, because this temple was entrusted to me. Only I can clean it up. The choice is mine.

I always laughed when I saw T-shirts that read, "You can have my chocolate when you pry it from my cold dead fingers." Yes, I'm one of those chocoholics who love it when some expert on TV tells me that chocolate is good for my heart or my blood pressure or my mood. I don't care how it's good for me as long as I can justify my addiction. This attitude is analyzed in one of Solomon's proverbs: "There is a way that seems right to a man, but in the end it leads to death" (Proverbs 14:12).

Old habits die hard, but I am working on it. I don't eat chocolate every day anymore. Sometimes I can go for weeks without a candy bar. Not that I don't think about them. But while I'm thinking about chocolate, I'm spreading peanut butter on a piece of whole-wheat bread and slicing some fruit to go with it. This snack contains a lot more nutrition than a candy bar, and the choice is entirely mine.

What does diet have to do with being a victor? Quite a bit, actually, because being a victor encompasses every aspect of our lives. Not only does diet affect how we look and feel physically, it also affects how we feel about ourselves—and victims have enough issues with self-esteem without making it harder. Making the choice to take control of one's diet is empowering. It's just another way to be an overcomer instead of a succumber.

If we were preparing to compete in the Olympics, we'd begin training well in advance of the actual competition. We'd be training 24/7. We'd be listening to our coach and our dietician and doing everything they recommended, because we know that if we have even a chance at winning a medal, we must be the very best that we can be.

Well, you're more than an athlete. You're a victor, and the race you're running is bigger than any marathon on earth. You've got the best coach and the best dietician in the universe, and He's written His instruction for you in one concise book, the Bible. Yes, the Bible says quite a bit about our diets. Grab a concordance sometime and do some research. You'll find it fascinating reading. God cares about every aspect of our lives. Wheaties may be the breakfast of champions, but the breakfast of victors is the Word of God.

You see, it's not just our physical food that I'm talking about. Just as important, we need to think about what we feed our minds. What we watch, what we read, what we listen to—all have an impact on our minds, our memories, and our motivation. If we don't fill our minds with things that inspire and edify us, we won't have anything inspiring to pull out when we need it.

The world is full of distractions. Satan plans all of that very carefully. His goal is to take up every precious moment of our day worrying about worldly needs, worldly cares, worldly obligations, worldly appetites, and worldly goals—anything to keep our eyes off Jesus. That way he keeps us focused on the world and off of Jesus with devices of our own making.

There are those who will argue that radio, television, and Internet service are wholly unfit for Christian consumption. But the reality is that the media are not harmful in themselves. Every one of these media offers some very fine Christian programming. Certainly, Christian and other family-appropriate material is the exception, but it is there, and it's up to us to seek out programs and sites that glorify God if we use those media. It's all in the choices we make.

I will throw in one warning here. Not all so-called Christian programs are based on truth. The devil just loves to throw a little poison into the Kool-Aid. We must be alert and not believe everything packaged as Christian unless we can back the teaching with the Scriptures. The Bible gives us guidelines: "To the law and to the testimony! If they do not speak according to this word, they have no light of dawn" (Isaiah 8:20). Unfortunately, many sincere people, even people in pastoral positions, don't know what the Scriptures say. We must be careful to weigh what we see and hear against the Scriptures and choose only the good.

The same discretion is needed for the music we listen to because its evil can be more subtle than visual evil. Without even thinking about it, we find ourselves mindlessly humming or singing along to a catchy tune. When we focus on the words, we realize that they have nothing to do with the Christian life at all.

On the other hand, when we start to listen to Christian music and find ourselves singing along to words like, "In God we trust for He is faithful. We put our trust in Him alone," we start growing spiritually. Our focus turns from the cares of this world and looks toward heaven. Once we make that connection, it stays with us for hours.

Like everything else, discernment gets better with practice. Spiritual tastes are acquired. We are creatures of habit, but habits can be changed. Such change takes effort, but it's worth every ounce of it.

Paul tells us to focus on the good stuff. "Whatever is true, whatever is noble, whatever is right, whatever is pure, whatever is lovely, whatever is admirable—if anything is excellent or praise-worthy—think about such things. Whatever you have learned or received or heard from me, or seen in me—put it into practice. And the God of peace will be with you" (Philippians 4:8, 9).

Obviously, this is quite a lifestyle change for some of us. We can make that change in a couple of ways. We can go cold turkey, or we can wean ourselves gradually as our discernment and conviction grow. But the cold-turkey method will involve further growth and more removal from that which is worldly.

Most newspapers, magazines, and novels are not going to feed our souls. They are just junk food that gives the sensation of fullness without the nutrition, and it's not going to sustain us through eternal life.

There's only one food with guaranteed spiritual nutrition. Read the Scriptures daily. Feed upon God's promises. Meditate on the life of Christ. Develop a deep and trusting relationship with your personal Savior, because it is that relationship that is going to save you. Then pack a snack in your mind to nibble on throughout the day.

"The LORD is my light and my salvation—whom shall I fear?" (Psalm 27:1).

"Your word is a lamp to my feet and a light for my path" (Psalm 119:105).

If reading the Bible seems awkward at first, start with the Gospels: Matthew, Mark, Luke, and John. They will introduce you to the Creator, who came to this earth to redeem us. Find out what He came to this earth to do for you. Study His compassion, His mercy, His love for the downtrodden. Put yourself into the story and live it.

If you need guides to help you begin studying the Scriptures, I can highly recommend the Discover Bible Guides that are designed to lead you through the Scriptures one subject at a time, allowing the Scriptures themselves to answer your questions. These guides are available by calling the Voice of Prophecy at (877) 955-2525. Or you can study online at <www.vop.com>. See? Here is evidence that even the Internet has its good sites. I can personally credit these guides with my own understanding of the Bible. The guides made it all come together in one complete picture and helped me fall in love with my Savior.

Proverbs 23:12 admonishes us to "apply your heart to instruction and your ears to words of knowledge." *Apply* means to put our whole hearts into it. Make this the number one focus in our lives.

Now that we know what we have to do, it's time to do some house cleaning. Let's start with the bookcase. How many of those books actually build you up as a victor in Christ? Make a discard pile of the ones that you simply cannot justify keeping. Romance novels, action adventures, and other fluff just fill you with fantasy and take up precious time that you don't have to spare.

Start replacing them with books that will strengthen your relationship with God. Books on prayer, books on the Holy Spirit, books about people who have had incredible and inspiring experiences, books that speak to your heart. The encouragement you gain from them will bolster you all day long. But never let even these books get in the way of your time alone with the Scriptures. Those other books are just appetizers to get your taste buds going. The Bible is the full meal.

Be sure to add a good Bible concordance and a Bible dictionary to your new library. You can invest some pretty good dollars in a set of Bible commentaries, too, but they are well worth the money. When you really start delving into the Scriptures, you'll appreciate these resources. You'll pay as much for that set of commentaries as you would for a second television for the bedroom. Trust me, if you have one television, you don't need another one.

Once you've got that bookcase looking good, head for the cabinet that holds your videocassettes and DVDs. This is going to be harder, but be brutally honest. Pretend that Jesus is right there next to you helping you decide. How many of them can you really justify keeping? How many of them do you even want to admit you own?

Don't be surprised when the ones you justify keeping become even less desirable as you develop your appetite for godly things. As you mature in your Christian walk, vulgar language you once shrugged off as part of normal everyday life will become offensive. So will some of those bedroom scenes. A trashcan is always nearby.

When you're finished with that cabinet, head over to your music collection and do the same thing. This one should be easier. You may justify keeping some perfectly good secular music, but you'll find that, as you grow closer to Christ, you'll lose your appetite for much of it. It will just seem so trivial. You'll truly appreciate the beauty in songs of praise.

Find a Christian radio station and keep the dial there. You'll get news to keep you abreast with the latest happenings, and all the weather reports you need. In between, you'll get wonderful thoughts to ponder that will deepen your trust in God, and you'll also learn to sing to the Lord outside of church. Pretty soon you'll be singing to Him every time you have a free moment. No more shallow songs about drinking and partying and staying out all night. No more wooing and woe-ing over lovers. There is One whose love is real, One who will never leave you and never break your heart. Sing your love songs to Him.

You may not have control over the radio where you work. If not, the Holy Spirit can help you to tune it out and keep your thoughts on uplifting things. It's a whole lot easier to do if you listen to Christian radio before you get there.

Besides Christian radio, you can listen to tapes or CDs on your way to work. You can get the entire Bible on cassette tapes or CDs. You even have a choice of translations. Balance them with some good Christian music, and by the time you get to work you will be praising the Lord and surrendering your will to Him. You will enter your workplace fully confident that there is nothing you and God can't accomplish together.

Long day at work? Do the same thing coming home, and all the cares of the day will pale in the light of God's promises. By the time you walk in the door, you'll be ready to give your dog, your kids, and your spouse the love they've all been waiting for. Then, instead of burying yourself in the newspaper, make sure you spend some family time together and pray together before you go to bed. The family that prays together stays together. That's just one more way to live like a victor. Why not make it an entire family of victors?

If you live alone, remember, you don't really. God doesn't invite us to spend time with Him only in church. He wants to live in our hearts and our homes every hour of every day. All we have to do is invite Him in. In those silent moments He is there.

As a society we are almost afraid of silence. We think we have to fill every minute of our lives with noise. We no longer know how to listen to the quiet and relish its peace, and we rob ourselves from hearing God's small voice inside us. The Bible says, " 'Be still, and know that I am God' " (Psalm 46:10).

Don't spend all your time with technology blaring words into your ears. Find some quiet time every day to spend in reflection of God's Word. Go to bed earlier so you can rise earlier and start your day with Him. Write your thoughts down and then listen to that still voice for guidance.

Most of us are free to do whatever we want during our lunch hour. Take your Bible to lunch. You'll find it the most interesting lunch date you've ever had. It may take some discipline on your part to change your lunch-hour habits, so I'd like to share a method that worked for me.

Several months ago, I made a decision to spend my lunch hour with the Bible, but every day when I went into the break room to eat my sack lunch, there was the morning newspaper calling me to read it instead. (Newspaper voices sound a lot like the devil, by the way.)

Now, there was nothing really wrong with reading the news-paper during my lunch hour. My boss even provided it for his employees to enjoy. The problem was that it robbed me of fifty-five precious minutes with God's Word that I could not get back. As I punched that time clock, I had just given my boss four faithful hours of service, and I would give him four more after lunch. This hour was for me, and the best way that I could spend it was with my Savior and look heavenward in the middle of my day.

But that newspaper was calling my name. I resisted the temp-tation by removing the newspaper, laying out my lunch and my Bible, and then bowing my head in prayer. I thanked God first for the peanut-butter sandwich and apple that would nourish me for the next few hours. And then I thanked Him for the spiritual feast that lay open before me, because it would feed me for eternity.

Jesus called Himself both the Living Water and the Bread of Life. Those who eat this Bread and drink this Water will never hunger or thirst again. When I recognized how much more important my Bible feast was than my simple lunch, I began to look at my lunch hour in a special way. I left that break room every afternoon feeling both well fed and fed well. Jesus said, "Blessed are those who hunger and thirst for righteousness, for they will be filled" (Matthew 5:6).

With all this talk about fitting God into our schedules morning, noon, and night, you'd think that it's all about quantity. It's not. It's all about spending quality time with the Word. We have a small group that meets on Tuesday nights. We may spend two and a half hours just pondering thoughts that come out of three or four verses from our study guide. It's not important to us how much ground we cover. It's far more important how deep we go in understanding all that the text has to say to us. We are not gulping our spiritual meal. We are savoring every morsel.

For instance, everyone in our group was well aware that Jesus was the Word who was made flesh and dwelt among us. We've read that in the first chapter of John more than once, but in a deeper study recently we learned just what "the Word" meant to the Greeks in Jesus' day.

For centuries the Greeks believed in a divine figure called "the Word" (*logos* in Greek). He was the creator and sustainer of the universe, the source of reason and intelligence, and the mediator between the great god and the creation. When John referred to Jesus as the Word, he was appealing to the Greeks in terms they could understand. Jesus not only fulfilled Bible prophecy for the Jews. He fulfilled the beliefs of the Greeks as well.

Think about what that means. Jesus was proclaiming the good news to all people. He came to save us all. I will never again read the title "the Word" without reflecting upon its expanded meaning.

It's time for us all to do more than invite Christ to live in our hearts. It's time to invite Him into every aspect of our lives. Don't treat Him like a guest who will leave in a few hours. Don't invite Him in and then ignore Him as if He isn't there. Make Him as important to you as you are to Him.

He waits to be wanted.

MY RESOLUTION

Starting now, I will invite Jesus into both my heart and my home. I will make Him as important to me as I am to Him. I will seek His guidance as I work at changing old habits, so that my new habits will focus more completely on my relationship with Him.

CHAPTER 11
DON'T ASK WHY

Dear friends, do not be surprised at the painful trial you are suffering, as though
something strange were happening to you.
But rejoice that you participate in the sufferings of Christ,
so that you may be overjoyed when his glory is revealed (1 Peter 4:12, 13).

Pamela's* life would have been entirely different if only she had been born a boy. Her two older brothers were the apple of their mother's eye. She dressed them in nice clothes, fed them well, and treated them to ice cream just for the fun of it. But not Pamela.

When she was still just a toddler, her father had taken an unhealthy interest in his little girl, and that made Pamela's mother incredibly jealous. To punish the child for taking her husband's affections away, Pamela's mother would lock her in the closet for hours. She was the "bad girl" who didn't deserve ice cream like her brothers.

Relatives noticed that when the family came for visits, the two boys were allowed to play like normal children. They came in to eat with the family at the big table. But Pamela was made to sit in the back of the family's pickup with the hot sun pouring down on the aluminum camper shell that covered it. Pamela was being punished for being "bad." Sometimes her Aunt Jackie would sneak a treat in to her. She noticed that Pamela's clothes always looked

*Not her real name.

dirty and were too small for her, such a contrast from the two boys.

By the time Pamela was three years old, her father was molesting her on a regular basis. Her mother had walked in on them more than once, but instead of seeing it as the abuse it was, she just resented the little girl for getting all the attention. Pamela was five years old when her mother packed up and moved out of the house, taking her two sons with her. If her husband wanted to give all his affection to Pamela, she would leave her to him.

Pamela spent the rest of her childhood moving from place to place to avoid nosy relatives and keep ahead of the rumors. She shared a bedroom with her father and was made to perform "favors" on demand. School was her only refuge, but she dared not tell her secrets to anyone. When she became a teenager, her father threatened to kill her if she dated. She belonged to him, and only him.

Pamela finally escaped her father when she turned eighteen and could legally move out of the house. Far too late to save her, their secrets were eventually revealed, and her father was sent to prison.

When I met Pamela, she was twenty-seven years old, married, with three little boys of her own. She's doing her best to be the kind of parent she wishes her own parents had been for her. She admits that her relationship with her husband is probably not as spontaneous as it could have been were it not for the abuse she suffered as a child. But counseling has helped her to understand what a healthy sexual relationship is supposed to be.

As she remembers, Pamela offers details of her abuse quite matter-of-factly, speaking from the viewpoint of a child and yet speaking of things that children shouldn't even have to know about at such a tender age. This is her reality, and there is nothing anybody can do to undo what has already been done. All she can do is go on from here, and that's exactly what she's doing.

For a mother to leave a child to be raised by an abusive father is unthinkable for most of us. Why didn't she rescue her own precious child? Why didn't authorities investigate relatives' suspicions? Why didn't somebody save that child?

Life is full of situations that don't make sense to us, and no amount of reasoning is going to make it so. Not everything that happens in life is fair. It just is. A lot of bad things happen to people who least deserve it. I can't think of anyone who would deserve being abused as Pamela was. But it doesn't change the fact that it happened.

The Bible tells us about a man who loved the Lord with all his heart. God had blessed him abundantly, and Job used his wealth to help those less fortunate than himself. Everyone who came into contact with him was blessed in some way, whether by his compassion, his generosity, or his faith in his heavenly Father. If ever there was a man who didn't deserve what happened to him, it was Job. And yet, a string of tragedies befell him that would bring any man to the brink of total despair.

It was bad enough that Job lost his entire livelihood when his livestock were stolen and killed, but that paled in comparison to the tragic deaths of all *ten* of his children. As if that weren't enough to destroy even the most faithful of God's people, the final blow was a case of terrible boils all over his body.

How much tragedy can one man endure? And why? Why was this happening to a man who loved and served the Lord with all his heart, who gave to the poor and took care of the widows and fatherless?

Job's friends surely didn't have the answer. Oh, they had all kinds of theories, all of them dead wrong. But not even Job understood why his entire life had crumbled in his hands. The ordeal left Job in deep despair. He wanted to just give up and die. But one thing that he wanted more than that was to be vindicated in God's eyes. He was certain that his integrity would stand before God.

God does reveal to us why it all happened. It was Satan who targeted Job to test his faithfulness in his relationship to God. In spite of all the tragedies, Job did stand firm. Satan lost that battle, and Job's testimony serves as a witness to us all that we can also stand firm in times of trouble.

But not everything that happens on this earth happens because of Satan's testing. Sometimes God tests us to discipline our characters so that we may be fit for His kingdom. The wise man advises, "My son, do not despise the LORD's discipline and do not resent his rebuke, because the LORD disciplines those he loves, as a father the son he delights in" (Proverbs 3:11, 12).

God looks at everything in light of eternity. Nothing is permanently lost here on earth, but it can be lost forever if we do not choose God now. A kingdom without sin demands discipline and obedience to God's laws of love.

Believe it or not, suffering actually serves a purpose. It teaches us to hate sin. In fact, one of the most important lessons we must learn here on earth is that life and happiness cannot reign where sin exists. We must learn to abhor sin for what it truly is, so that we will long for its destruction and look forward to a life free of it.

The apostle Peter explains the abhorrence this way: "Since Christ suffered in his body, arm yourselves also with the same attitude, because he who has suffered in his body is *done with sin*. As a result, he does not live the rest of his earthly life for evil human desires, but rather for the will of God" (1 Peter 4:1, 2, emphasis added).

Did you hear that? We are done with sin and want to live for the will of God. We've had enough of it, and we want to live free of it. That's exactly what God is preparing us to do. Jesus left two thousand years ago to prepare a place for us, and while we're waiting, the Holy Spirit is preparing us for the place!

But that's still not the only reason bad things happen on earth. This earth is a test tube, and sometimes we get caught up in the reaction when two active but opposite ingredients work against each other within the same vessel. Sometimes we just have to hold on to the rim and try to keep our heads above the surface. When sin overtakes the minds of others, too often innocent people fall victim to their evil desires. No, it's not fair. It just is.

But isn't God in control of the universe? Can't He stop this insanity? Yes, He can. But God must allow sin to run its course to its completion. If He stands in the way, Satan can accuse Him of not giving his way a fair trial. Above all, this battle is to vindicate God and His law of justice and love once and for all—not just before the world but also before the universe.

If we stand on His side of that battle, then that victory is also to vindicate us. We need to have no fear of the Judgment Day that will soon come upon the earth, because Jesus, our Advocate, stands not to condemn us but to defend us from the father of lies who accuses us day and night.

Satan stands before the jury of the universe and testifies that we are sinners unworthy of salvation. And he's correct. We are all sinners. Through one man—Adam—sin entered the world. And the wages of sin is death. But through one Man—Jesus Christ—we can all be saved. Jesus stands before the Father and offers His blood to atone for our sins. By the blood of the Lamb, we are saved. Case closed. Satan has no evidence to convict us if we cling to Christ as our victory.

When disaster strikes our lives, our major challenge is remembering that Christ has already won the victory. It's easy to praise the Lord and sing at the top of our lungs when life is full of sunshine. But if tragedy suddenly struck right now, many of us would struggle to remember that God is in control and that this tragedy is only temporary.

Some of us would immediately begin to struggle with the Why questions. Why did this happen to me? Why have I been singled out? What did I do to deserve this? If God loves me, why didn't He stop this from happening?

We get so lost in the circumstances, so lost in trying to make sense of the senseless, that we lose sight of the One who knows what's going on from beginning to end. We become victims to every circumstance we encounter.

The greatest tragedy in our suffering comes when we turn away from God, when we blame Him for the things that Satan is responsible for. In some ways George and I know how that feels. On the night that our children were killed, we were treated as suspects in their murders. How could anyone possibly have thought that we would have wanted our own children to die? Surely we were the last people on earth who wanted that to happen.

That's a glimpse into how God feels, and yet so often He gets the blame when bad things happen to *His children*.

When I was eleven years old, my eight-year-old cousin died of leukemia. My family had started going to church with my uncle's family after Crystal was diagnosed. It was our family's attempt to seek comfort in God in the midst of the tragedy. But after Crystal died, we quit going to church. My uncle said he couldn't love a God that would let his little girl die. So our church-going days ended almost as quickly as they began. My family's entire faith rested on healing, and when it didn't come, they gave up on God.

So many people pray for healing or other miracles and then lose faith when it doesn't come. The Bible tells us to pray without ceasing, but what good are prayers if God doesn't answer them?

The day before our oldest daughter, Stephanie, died of cancer, I was so angry watching her in pain that I stomped down to the hospital chapel and told God, "You heal her now, or You take her now. She can't take any more pain!" Twelve hours later Stephanie slipped away.

Did God take her life because healing was impossible? Nothing is impossible for God. While on earth Jesus healed people. He even raised some of them from the dead. Why didn't He do that for Stephanie? Hadn't we lost enough already? Couldn't He have spared just one of our children?

We need to be assured that if we ask, God will grant healing for those who trust Him. But for many, healing will not happen until Jesus returns to earth to take us home.

Yes, Jesus healed and raised the dead back to life, but most of those people had to wait until Jesus came to them—or they to Him. Most of us will also have to wait to see His face coming in the clouds before we receive our healing.

Occasionally, God does answer prayers with miracles. But mostly He relies on us to hang in there with Him until the time is right—and only He knows when that time will be. If we could pull the curtain back so that we could see the cosmic battle raging behind the scenes, we would all agree that God has good reason to hold off.

Our most heartfelt prayer should be that all of God's children will be saved, that not just our families, but God's entire family will turn to Him and be ready for His coming.

I'm ready to go home. I'm ready to hold my children again. And sometimes I grow mighty weary of the wait. But I'm going to hang in there, because God has other children that He wants to save. And some of them aren't ready to go home yet. Only He knows how much time we each need to accept His offer of salvation.

The Bible assures us that God is not willing that anyone should perish but that all should come to repentance. (See 2 Peter 3:9.) Too often it takes a tragedy to bring sinners to their knees. Too often we must face death itself before we will recognize our need for a Savior.

When bad things happen, the point is not to analyze why this has happened to us, but to reach that point in our lives where we can say, "Now that this has happened, how will I respond to it? How can I use this experience to both grow spiritually closer to Christ and shake my fist at the devil?"

The victory over the devil is won daily in all the decisions we make and how we respond to the sin around us. Every day we can shake our fist at the devil. But we need to make sure that armor is tight around us. The devil does not fight fair!

The Bible says, "We are hard pressed on every side, but not crushed; perplexed, but not in despair; persecuted, but not abandoned; struck down, but not destroyed." For all of these troubles are light and momentary, "achieving for us an eternal glory that far outweighs them all" (2 Corinthians 4:8, 9, 17).

MY RESOLUTION

From here on out, when bad things happen, I will not ask why. Instead I will say, "Now that this has happened, how will I respond to it? How can I use this experience to both grow spiritually closer to Christ and shake my fist at the devil?"

CHAPTER 12
COME OUT SHINING

He knows the way that I take; when he has tested me,
I will come forth as gold (Job 23:10).

If the scars left behind by tragedy are Purple Hearts, then Tammy Harris is clothed from head to toe in purple. But when I look at Mark and Tammy Harris, I don't see purple. I see gold!

Mark and Tammy are two of the most beautiful people I have ever met. You have to take the time to get to know them, and you have to be willing to look beyond the surface to see it. But once you've heard their story, you'll understand just how beautiful they are in the eyes of God.

Mark and Tammy have literally been tried in the fire and have come out shining. Even as children, they both knew that they were gold. Both of their families had raised them to know and love the Lord as their personal Savior.

At twenty-one, Mark was already serving as a youth leader in the Springerville, Arizona, Seventh-day Adventist Church. He was excited about his ministry because he felt he was truly making an impact on nearly twenty young lives.

Tammy was nineteen and lived in Kingman, Arizona, on the other side of the state. She, too, was actively involved in her church and had just come back from a mission trip in Mexico. She and

Mark had made plans for her to come to Springerville and spend two weeks with Mark's family, so the two could get to know each other better. Little did Tammy know that Mark had plans to propose to her while she was visiting in Springerville.

Tammy and Mark had spent the past few days together shopping, skiing, and just having fun. But now it was Sabbath, and the family rose early to arrive in time for Mark's dad to warm the church before services and for Mark to set up for his youth meeting. The day was January 5, 1985.

The youth group met in a tiny building adjacent to the church. As Mark's father headed into the church, Mark hurried to the youth building to prepare his lesson materials and tune his guitar. Upon entering the building, he noticed that it was quite chilly inside. He went to the furnace to investigate. The pilot light had gone out.

Tammy had just entered the building and was standing by the door with it still slightly ajar when Mark lit the match. Neither of them knew that propane gas had been building up on the floor. When Tammy opened the door to enter, the gas headed straight for the exit, and Tammy was standing right in its path.

The flash blew right past Mark and engulfed Tammy from head to toe. Mark tried frantically to beat the flames from Tammy's clothes, but her fake fur jacket provided the perfect tinder. Together they reached for the door to pry it open, but the blast had pulled the walls away from the foundation and jammed the door tightly shut.

Mark's mother and sister heard the explosion and headed for the youth building. Together they yanked the door open and pulled the couple out of the inferno. Their clothes hung in shreds on their bodies. The lace collar from Tammy's dress had burned completely away, leaving its pattern around her neck.

Later Mark's mother would insist that she did not make it to the door in time to help her daughter open it. She was behind her by several steps and could not keep up. Mark's sister insists that she was there, and the two pried the door open together. It was jammed so tightly that she knew she could not have done it alone. As they look back, both of them believe that an angel stepped in and opened the door for them.

Mark and Tammy were life-flighted to a hospital in Phoenix, where a brand-new state-of-the-art trauma center had just opened its doors. Every other burn unit in the state was at capacity.

By the time they arrived, Tammy's head had swollen to the size of a basketball and her eyes were swollen shut. Her own mother did not recognize her. She was burned nearly from head to toe. Tammy had told several nurses and doctors that she had contact lenses in but no one seemed to be willing to take them out for her. Later, doctors would determine that the contact lenses probably saved her eyes from the flash. Her clothing had not been so kind. Nearly everything she had been wearing was made of synthetic fabric and had melted to her.

Memories of that first week are fuzzy for both of them. Except for severe damage to his hands, Mark's injuries were mostly internal. The flames had been sucked into his throat, esophagus, and lungs. Tubes were inserted to keep open the airways, but as his body responded to the burns, damaged tissue would break away in his airway and threaten to suffocate him. Twice in that first week Mark nearly died. Down the hall, Tammy was also fighting for her life.

Tammy's injuries were mostly external, and the damage was severe. She had been given eleven pints of blood to replace what was lost when layers of skin were burned away, exposing muscles and tendons.

The doctors had tried a new procedure of applying an artificial skin to her chest in hopes of protecting the exposure until her body could regenerate new skin. Her system reacted violently to the new skin and infection rapidly set in. With a temperature of 104 degrees, Tammy was rushed into surgery to remove the artificial skin and try to arrest the infection, but the doctors truly didn't expect her to come out of it alive.

Apparently God had plans for Mark and Tammy. Against all odds, they both survived. The next several months were filled with surgeries, skin grafts, whirlpool baths, and débridement sessions.

Both were made to wear tight-fitting bandages over the burned areas. Mark's hands grew webs between his fingers and began to close into fists. Surgery cut the webs loose, and Mark began excruciating therapy in hopes of saving the mobility in his hands.

Tammy wore a specially made mask and a horribly restrictive neck brace. Among her biggest challenges was learning to walk all over again.

At times, Mark lost hope and just wanted to give up. His feelings of guilt overwhelmed him as he thought constantly of what Tammy was going through. But something inside of Tammy told her she was going to recover. Even inside the youth building, with her body engulfed in flames, she had been filled with peace. As Mark had worked furiously to beat away the flames, she had kept saying, "I'm OK. I'm going to be fine."

As the weeks progressed and Mark was able to get out of bed, he would go to Tammy's room, put her in a wheelchair, and take her out to explore the halls of the twenty-story hospital. With his hands in bandages, he steered Tammy's wheelchair with his elbows, and the two young adventurers set out on their own personal journey together. Before long, the intercom would announce, "Mark and Tammy, your nurses are looking for you. Please return to your rooms."

While Mark thought of Tammy every waking moment, Tammy knew in her heart that she had to release Mark from their relationship. She felt sorrier for other people than she did for herself because they had to look at her. Tammy could still see herself from the inside, and she knew she was still a beautiful person. She determined to let that beauty shine in her attitude for all to see. But it wasn't right to hold on to Mark; he deserved someone who was still beautiful on the outside.

Mark had different feelings. As he watched Tammy's valiant efforts to overcome the tragedy, he saw strengths in her character of which he had been unaware. If anything, the tragedy had tied the knot even tighter, and Mark knew for certain that Tammy was the woman with whom he would spend the rest of his life. Three months after the tragedy, Mark proposed and Tammy accepted. A year later they were wed.

Challenges continued for the young couple. Tammy was told she would not be able to have children. Her skin lacked the elasticity to stretch during pregnancy. But for Tammy, the *T* stood for tenacity, and she set out to prove the doctors wrong. Her God was bigger than this, and if He wanted them to have a child, they would have one.

On November 5, 1990, Tammy gave birth to a beautiful baby girl. They named her Angela. In answer to prayer, Tammy's skin had stretched. She had carried Angela to term and delivered her naturally. Now Tammy set out to prove the doctors wrong once again. She would breastfeed her baby successfully. On April 8, 1994, the doctors would place a son in her arms; the second pregnancy was as uneventful as the first.

Today, the lives of the Harris family are happy and full. Mark and Tammy are both actively involved in youth ministry at the Hamilton, Montana, Seventh-day Adventist Church. They lead nearly thirty children in Pathfinder activities, and they are an inspiration to us all.

I had the privilege of teaching the Harris children at the Blodgett View Christian School, and they are just two of the kids I have bonded with and now call my own. You cannot look at Angela and Matthew without noticing the reflection of their parents in their bright faces. In them we catch a glimpse of the outside beauty their mother once had.

Mark and Tammy will carry the physical scars of their tragedy to the grave. Tammy's feet will forever carry the strap marks from her sandals; her neck will forever wear the pattern of the lace collar that decorated her dress. Her face will forever carry the scars left by flames that Mark so frantically tried to smother with his own now permanently scarred hands. No amount of surgery will undo the damage or restore their skin to its youthful beauty.

But when we gaze at the inner beauty that still shines from Tammy's brown eyes, and when we see the love that Mark's eyes reflect when he looks at his wife, we know that both of them are truly gold. They are gold tried in fire, and they have come out shining.

I asked them if they ever pondered why this might have happened to them. Mark has probably pondered it more than Tammy, but neither one of them ever blamed God for a moment, and they are secure in the knowledge that God knows all things.

Mark wonders if maybe Satan knew about some great thing that they were supposed to do and tried to snuff them out before it could happen. His youth ministry had been such an important part of his young life, and he has not let the tragedy keep him from that mission. But Mark doesn't see any special talents in himself or his wife that might have been such a threat to the devil. Perhaps it happened so that their children would not be born. Maybe it is their children who were destined to do great things for the Lord in these last days.

Whatever the reason, Mark and Tammy have shaken their fist at adversity and refused to give up. They are light in a dark world. Their faith is gold reflecting the pure love of their Savior for all to see.

We, too, can shine like gold tried in the fire. We, too, can reflect the love of the Savior for all the world to see. It was on the cross of affliction that Christ's love shone the brightest. It is in bearing our own afflictions that we, too, can rise to the challenge, allow the dross to be burned away, and come out shining.

MY RESOLUTION

When God looks at me, He sees gold. From here on, no matter what happens to me, I will do my best to reflect the love of the Savior and shine for Him.

CHAPTER 13
ONLY I CAN MAKE ME MAD

Better a patient man than a warrior, a man who controls his temper than one who takes a city (Proverbs 16:32).

It was a typical playground scuffle. Yes, it happens in Christian schools too. There was no real violence. One student shoved another and called the smaller one a derogatory name relating to his height, and the injured party came running to me expecting his teacher to set things right.

The offender received a short lecture on doing unto others and got to run three laps around the playground. The injured party learned a lesson that I had learned quite some time ago: Only I can make me mad.

The lesson had taken quite a while for me to learn. Having been raised by a father who solved everything with his temper, I had much to learn about anger management. Fortunately, God had seen fit to yoke me up with a peace-loving man who knew how to solve his issues with tact and diplomacy. Eight years on the police force had taught him how to diffuse a heated situation before it blew up. My husband has now been my teacher for thirty years, and a lot that he has tried to teach me is finally beginning to take root.

If the lesson was good for me, I reasoned, surely it would be good for my students. I pulled the teary fifth-grader close to me, put my arm around his shoulder, and recited the words, "Only I can make me mad."

"He's just trying to get to you," I explained. "If you don't let him get to you, you win! That's his whole goal: to make you mad. I'm challenging you to be the bigger man, and that has nothing to do with how tall you are. If instead of getting mad, you let his words just go in one ear and out the other, then all of his efforts are in vain. And then, if you come and tell a teacher what he's done, you not only win, but he loses, because he's out there running laps!

"Pretty soon he'll realize that it's not fun to tease you anymore, and he'll stop trying to make you mad, because he couldn't upset you. You win. He loses, because only I can make me mad."

This was not the only student who received this little lesson. Word began to spread, and soon I had students come back to me and say, "Mrs. Swift, I did what you told me and it works! Only I can make me mad."

Try as we might, we can't protect our children from all the pain that life has in store for them. We've got to build fortitude in them now because a time is coming when we will have to face some pretty unattractive situations in the name of the Lord. Do we want our kids to be victims or victors?

Certainly this lesson is not just for children. It's a lesson for us all. We live in such a thin-skinned society that people can actually be sued for saying something derogatory about another. Is that really right? What is it doing to our fortitude as a nation?

No matter what happens, no matter what anybody does to me, I'm the one responsible for my emotions, and only I can make me mad. If I cave in to my own emotions and let someone else get to me, I let him make me a victim.

As a victor, I have vowed not to let that happen. So you see how important this little lesson becomes. If I don't succumb to irrational emotions in a given situation, I stand as a victor instead of a victim. Whatever it is, I can choose to meet the challenge and rise above it. I can use everyday irritations to build my fortitude now. So that someday when the real time of trouble comes for all of us "who keep the commandments of God, and have the testimony of Jesus Christ," I'll have the fortitude to hold my emotions in check and stand up to it (Revelation 12:17, KJV).

I had a chance to practice recently at a gas station just blocks from my home. My husband had just filled our van with gas, so I headed into the station to pay.

"Eighteen dollars on number nine," I said as I handed the cashier my debit card.

The cashier swiped the card and pulled the receipt out for me to sign. The color drained from his face as he realized his mistake.

"I'm sorry, Ma'am," he said. "Another customer's charges hadn't been deleted, and I rang up his purchases with yours. I can fix it. It'll only take a minute."

"Not a problem," I told him. "I worked retail for nine years. I made mistakes too."

Obviously the young man wasn't in the habit of making this mistake because he hadn't memorized the steps necessary to delete a transaction. He tried once, twice, three times. And then he called his supervisor and explained the situation to her.

She wasn't real sure about the procedure either, so the two tried various options at the machine.

"How much more is it?" I asked, thinking maybe if it wasn't much it would be easier on all concerned to just refund me in cash. If it was too much, I didn't really want it taken out of my account. I also knew that the credit card companies take a certain percent of the purchase. That wouldn't be fair to the station.

The cashier grimaced. "It's over fifty dollars. I'm really sorry this is taking so long."

"Hey, it's OK," I assured him. "I'm in no hurry. Take your time."

Finally the machine registered all the right moves and popped out a ticket with a negative number on it. The cashier quickly reran the original $18.00 and presented me with three receipts, explaining each one. I signed them and took my copies.

"Thanks for being so nice about it," the cashier said. "Most people would have been really mad."

"Well," I said to him as I headed for the door. "Only I can make me mad. Hope the rest of the day goes easier for you."

I thought about that as I headed back to the van. Most people would have been really mad. Why are we so quick to attack others with anger? The cashier hadn't targeted me to try to make me miserable. In fact, the situation made him more uncomfortable than it did me. Sure, it took a few precious minutes from my life that I'll never get back again. But if that's the worst thing that happens to me today, I can sure handle that! Ecclesiastes 7:8 reminds us, "The end of a matter is better than its beginning, and patience is better than pride."

What impact did I have on that young cashier, his supervisor, and the customers around me? Were those really minutes lost in my life, or were they minutes well spent as a witness to others? I like to think it was the latter.

Someday, when we've passed all these tests and we're finally standing in the kingdom, how many people will come up to you and tell you a story about a positive impact you made on their lives? Think about that the next time you are tempted to act like "most people." You and I both know that we've got a higher calling. Because you and I are victors—and we know how to act like it.

"A man's discretion makes him slow to anger, and it is his glory to overlook a transgression" (Proverbs 19:11, NASB).

MY RESOLUTION

From now on, I will control my anger instead of letting my anger control me. Only I can make me mad.

CHAPTER 14
PATIENCE MAKES PERFECT

Consider it pure joy, my brothers, whenever you face trials of many kinds, because you know that the testing of your faith develops perseverance. Perseverance must finish its work so that you may be mature and complete, not lacking anything (James 1:2–4).

I had been on the job only two weeks, and we had a deadline to meet. A photography studio had ordered 800 flannel blankets covered with silk flowers to photograph children lying in a "bed of roses." The order called for a total of thirty-three roses to be sewn onto twelve fifteen-inch square panels that would then be attached to a flannel blanket. That meant 396 roses to a blanket. We were up to our eyeballs in over 300,000 silk roses, each with a tiny "Made in China" label that had to be removed before we could sew it on.

Everyone else had been working on this project for several months, and they were tired of it. Sewing-machine operators, flower sorters, blanket assemblers—every one of them just wanted to get this job finished and take a break! The fact that Christmas was fast approaching didn't make it any easier. Everyone wanted to go shopping, decorate their houses, bake cookies, and attend Christmas pageants. Everyone's minds seemed to be everywhere but here.

I was new blood, and I was enthusiastic about rising to the challenge and meeting this deadline head-on. Time was already against us. Every step had taken longer than Chris, the owner, had anticipated. As that December 19 deadline loomed closer on our horizon, the pace grew frantic in the shop.

My choleric personality was a natural for this kind of circumstance. I am a planner, an implementer, a delegator, a doer, and a motivator. I took it upon myself to set high goals of accomplishment. I might not be the fastest sewing-machine operator in this outfit, but I would be the very best that I could be.

It didn't take long for my attitude to begin to infect the entire shop. There were a few who plodded along at their steady pace, but others fed off of my energy and kicked it into high gear with new enthusiasm. I was the motivator!

To be a good motivator, you have to be able to read other people's personalities and use what works to motivate them.

One veteran operator could sew like the wind. She had trained me for this project, and I watched every step carefully to make sure I did mine in the most efficient way I could. My boss was paying me by the hour, and I wanted to make sure she got her money's worth.

The veteran was being paid by the piece, which, at the rate she sewed, was a better deal for her. But Connie had a hard time staying in her seat. When she was sitting, she was producing, but when she was standing, she was not.

I learned that Connie had a highly competitive spirit. So I used that to motivate her. I set my production goal high. Not so high that it wasn't attainable, but high enough to have to stretch for it. Then I challenged Connie to a friendly competition to see who could produce the most panels by the end of the day. Connie rose to the challenge and beat me by three. The boss was thrilled. Previously, Connie had been able to produce forty panels in a shift. That day she produced fifty-three. The competition exploded from there, as fellow employees cheered us to even higher goals. By the end of the week we had both topped sixty, and we stayed there until the project was complete. We were the A-team!

With our frenzied pace, even wolfing down our lunches and literally running to the bathroom so as not to waste precious time, the word *patience* simply didn't seem to fit into the picture at all. Patience to me meant slowing down, stopping, waiting. I wasn't thinking along those lines at all.

And so it caught me completely by surprise when I scurried past the boss working on the slowest machine in the shop and heard her call after me with complete frustration in her voice. "Joy, are you a patient person?"

The question stopped me in my tracks. For two weeks my goal had been to motivate this crew's attitude toward fast, efficient production. We were no longer machine operators; we *were* machines, well oiled and running at top speed.

I turned back to Chris and stuttered a reply. "Not really," I said. "That's one lesson God's really been working on with me. But I haven't got it perfect yet."

She looked up at me and laughed. "Neither do I," she said. "And this machine tacks so slowly that I'm about to throw it out the window."

I nodded my head in sympathy. "You got my vote," I told her. "I'm glad it's you working on that machine and not me. That one just might throw me over the edge, and then God would have to start all over with me."

As I sat back down to my machine, I began to ponder just where patience fits into even the most frenzied situation. There were several things that happened when we were sewing that threatened to slow us down and decrease our production. Our bobbin would run out of thread and have to be replaced, or the needle would break or come unthreaded, and we'd have to rethread it. The last one was the most frequent and frustrating.

As the pace grew more intense and the competition continued between Connie, me, and sometimes the boss when she could get on a faster machine, those little disruptions were felt intensely. I had been very careful about displaying a victor's attitude throughout this job, and I wasn't about to let these little disruptions get the best of me.

So I made up a word, and every time someone heard me say, "rassa-frassa" through gritted teeth, they'd start asking, "Lose your thread, Joy?"

"Nope," I'd answer. "It was the bobbin this time."

Pretty soon others were verbally expressing their disruptions in equally harmless ways. In doing so we built a team spirit. Recognizing that all of us were experiencing the same frustrating disruptions somehow made it easier. Some of the employees even learned ways to vent that frustration without resorting to profanity.

Profanity not only dishonors God in name, it dishonors the character He is building in us. Profanity is usually tied to a lack of patience and an inability to cope. When we resort to profanity, we're as good as admitting defeat. We victors are not so easily defeated.

Years ago, I used to tell people that I was put on this earth to learn patience, and I'm a very unwilling student. I had come to this conclusion because it seemed that I was constantly being confronted with circumstances that demanded patience for a gracious resolution. True to my words, I fought those lessons tooth and nail. I was not a patient person, and God was just going to have to learn to love me as I was.

Fortunately, I have an incredibly patient heavenly Father who loves me with all His heart. He has never given up on me. He just kept putting those patience lessons right there in front of me, until one day the light finally went on.

"You know, Joy," a wee small voice inside me said, "if you'd quit fighting these lessons and start paying attention and actually try to grasp the concept, you just might reach a point where I don't have to keep flinging them in your path."

Well, that was a monumental thought! So I started paying attention. I started pondering this patience issue and why it seemed so important to God that I learn it. Even I, a planner, doer, get-it-done kind of personality, needed patience to cope with everything life threw at me. It wasn't enough for me to accept the way I was; I had to strive to make myself better. And because patience fit my personality so poorly, I had to work even harder at it.

So now, as I walk through life, I look for ways that I can build patience. That's part of rising to the challenge. The illustration in the previous chapter about waiting for the gas-station attendant shows that not only have I been working on my anger issues, but I've been making huge progress on my patience issues, too.

A few days after my boss asked me if I was a patient person, a conversation arose about a radio news report on a pedophile and how each of us would administer justice. Talking out of character, I expressed agreement with another employee's views. One of the flower sorters seemed shocked that I would agree.

"Why, Joy," she said. "I could never see you hurting someone else. It's just not your character."

I looked straight at her and laughed.

"Thank you," I said. "Unfortunately, I am my father's daughter. My natural tendency is to want to do just what he taught me: to solve everything with my mouth and my fists. But God's really been working on me, and He's made incredible progress. I'm still my father's daughter, only now I look to my heavenly Father. Thank you for noticing the progress He's made in me."

Revealing to my co-workers that my character was not born in me, but was rather the work of God's Spirit in me was an incredible lesson in what God can do for any of us if we will just pay attention and surrender our natural wills to Him. What a witness for God's character we can be. That people can see our actions and hear the words that come out of our mouths and see God's reflection in front of them. There is no deeper honor than that.

Paul prayed that the Roman Christians be blessed with patience: "May the God of patience and comfort grant you to be like-minded toward one another, according to Christ Jesus, that you may with one mind and one mouth glorify the God and Father of our Lord Jesus Christ" (Romans 15:5, 6, NKJV).

The Bible warns us there is a time of trouble coming unlike anything we've previously encountered. Of all the attributes that God could point out in those who successfully endure it, patience is one of the three He chooses. "Here is the patience of the saints; here are those who keep the commandments of God and the faith of Jesus" (Revelation 14:12, NKJV).

Patience, obedience, faith. Those are the three attributes we need to work on the most if we are to stand in the last days and see our Savior coming to take us home. We won't be ready for the final test unless we've passed the pre-tests. This is God's classroom, and unless we buckle down and take our studies seriously, we will not pass through to the next level. We will flunk. And there will be no second chance.

"God is not unjust; he will not forget your work and the love you have shown him as you have helped his people and continue to help them. We want each of you to show this same diligence to the very end, in order to make your hope sure. We do not want you to become lazy, but to imitate those who *through faith and patience* inherit what has been promised" (Hebrews 6:10–12, emphasis supplied).

That's how important it is for us to learn patience. Our salvation depends on it.

I am convinced that this was the very attribute that King David lost as he grew older. I say *lost* because as a shepherd, he surely had it in his youth. One cannot tend sheep day in and day out without developing patience.

The demands of kingship must have changed David. When we read the psalms, we see nothing wrong with David's faith. He has no problem giving all of his problems to the Lord. But when we read those psalms in which he cries out to the Lord for help, wondering if God will ever come to his rescue, we are witnessing God's using David's own petitions and prayers to teach him patience. Because God knows just how important patience was to David's salvation.

God always answered David's prayers, but until David was willing to pay attention to the lessons, God would make David wait upon Him. Without patience, our faith will not stand long enough to resist the devil's lies. Start paying attention to the lessons on patience. Develop it to perfection, and God will be able to answer your prayers and petitions more quickly.

Even if He doesn't answer within your time frame, you will have the patience to endure the wait. The Bible says a thousand years is like a day to God. When He makes us wait for months to receive His answer, think about how short that is to Him. In light of eternity, it is just a flash in time.

In some versions of the Bible, the word *patience* is often translated as "perseverance" or "patient endurance." Those terms fit more comfortably with my personality because, to me, they speak less of slowing down, stopping, and waiting, and more of actively doing something. Patience is not just passively waiting; it is actively enduring the wait. For those of us who have lost loved ones and wait for Christ to come to reunite us, we are not patiently waiting. We are patiently enduring the wait. When Jesus hung on that cross, He didn't wait patiently to die. He endured the pain and anguish as He waited. When we are going through trials, we need patient endurance to keep our faith, obey God's will, and just get through it.

When someone is experiencing a tough time, I have the habit of saying, "Hang in there, Little Buckaroo." What that saying really means is, have patience. Persevere. Endure for just a little while longer, and this, too, shall pass. Isn't that what we'll all have to do to get through that time of trouble?

My greatest trial on earth demands patience from me. It's been more than twenty-five years since I last held five of my children. It's not easy for any parent to wait that long. But with my personality, the test is even harder. I have to wait, and there's nothing I can do to make the waiting shorter. Jesus will come when God the Father tells Him it is time. That's the day I will hold my children in my arms again. Not one moment before.

There are things that I can do to keep busy while I wait. Productive things. Things that will build my character, inspire others, and help us all draw closer to the Lord before that day. That's what makes the waiting easier for me. When it's all over, if I can stand before God and, with integrity, account for the time I spent waiting, I will have waited like a victor.

Sometimes I have to throw my own words right back in my own face. If I can endure waiting to hold the kids for as long as I have, shouldn't these little daily patience lessons be a piece of cake in comparison? Why, yes, they should. Then what's the problem?

Rise to the challenge and wait. Wait upon the Lord, and He shall renew your strength. He will lift you up on wings like eagles'.

If we can just learn to be patient, we can soar!

MY RESOLUTION

Since patience is so vital to my salvation, I'll take the lessons more seriously. With patient endurance, I will finish this race. I will wait upon the Lord, and I will soar.

CHAPTER 15
THE HARDEST STEP OF ALL

"When you stand praying, if you hold anything against anyone,
forgive him, so that your Father in heaven may forgive you your sins"
(Mark 11:25).

Forgiveness is a tough topic, especially for those of us who have fallen victim under the hands of another. I'm not going to pretend that forgiveness is easy. In fact, I think it's downright impossible if we try to do it on our own.

I mentioned the subject only briefly in a previous chapter because I didn't want anybody grabbing God's armor and setting out to beat the daylights out of their victimizers. I also knew that at the early stage of your transformation, you probably weren't ready to hear what I have to say now. Most likely you would have tuned me out, thrown this book in the trash, and gone right back into your self-made fortress.

It is useless to spring the idea of forgiveness on victims in the depth of their pain. I speak from experience because that's exactly what happened to George and me.

For several hours at the police station, while George was being questioned, I was left alone in a room with a Protestant minister. My anger had reached its boiling point. How could anyone just walk into my house and shoot my children? The words spewed out of my mouth. "Why can't I find the ones who did this and string them up and shoot them a thousand times? Doesn't the Bible say 'an eye for an eye'?"

I wanted justice, and I wanted it immediately. Administering it myself felt just fine to me. But the minister didn't agree with me.

"Joy," he said, "you should feel sorry for the ones who did this to your children, for someday they will feel the wrath of God."

"Sorry!" I spat back at him. "Why should I feel sorry for them? They're murderers! Feel sorry for my children. Feel sorry for me!"

Hours later, George was left alone with this same minister. Oddly, George asked him the same question and was told, "You should get down on your knees and beg forgiveness for whoever did this."

As I did, George completely shut him out. The minister had lost us. He demanded something of us that we could not yet do.

That was a long time ago, and yet I remember every word the minister said; the impact on me was so huge because the timing was so wrong. It takes time for us to reach that point in our healing where we can even talk about the issue of forgiving our trespassers because for some of us that trespass was just too big. We've been too violated; our loss is too great.

For years I worked on my healing by building my faith in God. I learned to pray and to give all my troubles to Him. I learned to trust Him, to worship Him, and to praise His name even in the midst of my trials.

The first time I read Mark 11, I clung to the promise in verses 22 through 24. " 'Have faith in God,' Jesus answered. 'I tell you the truth, if anyone says to this mountain, "Go, throw yourself into the sea," and does not doubt in his heart but believes that what he says will happen, it will be done for him. Therefore I tell you, whatever you ask for in prayer, believe that you have received it, and it will be yours.' "

I loved this promise of faith! I clung to it with all my heart. But when I read the next verse, I wanted to reject the whole thing. " 'When you stand praying, if you hold anything against anyone, forgive him, so that your Father in heaven may forgive you your sins' " (Mark 11:25).

This was a foul ball! It was telling me that if I didn't forgive my trespassers, God wouldn't forgive me. That was not fair. The scales were not equal. Nothing I had ever done and needed forgiveness for even came close to what those two boys did to me.

I hated this verse because it demanded something of me that I could not do. I threw it under a rock and walked away. I could not deal with it.

True to His character, God kept pulling it out and throwing it back in my path. For years He did that, until one day I fell to my knees and asked God to show me how I could possibly forgive. He answered me right away. He gave me a perspective that, as a parent, I could understand.

I have eight children, and I love every one of them with all my heart. There is nothing they could ever do to make me stop loving them. When they are kind and considerate and loving, especially toward one another, it makes me so proud of them.

But sometimes they're mean. Sometimes they hurt each other! And that hurts me because I want my children to love each other as much as I love each one of them. Unfortunately, on earth we have sibling rivalry, and my children, being sinful and self-centered by nature, have a hard time loving each other that way.

Still, I love them unconditionally, and that's exactly how our heavenly Father feels about us. We're His children, and there is nothing we could do that would ever make Him stop loving us and longing for our salvation.

God watched as my children, *His* children, were gunned down that night. He saw the injustice of their deaths. But He also watched His own young sons pulling the trigger, and He cried for them, as well. In some ways He may have even cried harder for them, because their actions could cost them eternal life.

In light of eternity, God knew that the deaths of the other four were only temporary. He had sent His Son 2,000 years before to die on a cross that they might share in His death and win the victory in His resurrection.

But it would take a truly repentant heart to save the other two, and Satan would do his best to maintain his control on the hearts of God's two sons. These two, God may lose forever.

The thought of losing even one of my own children forever is more than I can bear. How can a God of love feel anything less? And so I began looking at forgiveness through the eyes of my Father. I realized that only through repentance and forgiveness could God's sons be saved—but not just those two sons. Without repentance and forgiveness, not one of God's children could be saved. Not even mine. Not even me.

Wow! Now I began to understand. I am God's child. I am part of His family. And I don't want to lose any of us.

Yes, I have every right in the world to hate what Billy and Ray did to my family one foggy night in 1977. We did nothing to provoke them. We were completely innocent of any wrongdoing toward them, and we were victimized by their actions.

But if I am to be counted among the sons and daughters of God, I must be willing to love all of God's children the way He loves each of us. I must be willing to love the sinner and hate the sin.

When you think about it, even from a victim's standpoint, it all begins to make sense. If we rise above the tragedy and genuinely forgive the perpetrators, we turn the tragedy into a victory for us. We are no longer their victims. We are victors instead.

Now I am not going to pretend that that's an easy thing to do. It took me about a decade to get there myself, and my husband is just now coming to grips with it after twenty-six years. But the day I forgave Billy and Ray, I quit being their victim.

The same holds true for the victims they killed. If Christ's sacrifice was sufficient to save my children, then the grave has no hold on them. The victory is already theirs. Yes, we have to wait to see the final results, but that victory is sure.

So now the only victims in this entire situation are the perpetrators themselves, because they fell victim to the great deceiver, and in the process they have lost eternal life.

Or have they?

If God loves all His children unconditionally, as I love mine, then even the perpetrators are welcome in the kingdom, *if* they turn away from their sins and cling to Jesus Christ. They must repent. They must, with a contrite heart, surrender their lives to Christ. But isn't that what we all must do?

The victory belongs to all of us if only we will grab hold of it and refuse to let go. In Christ, nobody has to end up a victim. Today, right now, we can all be victors in Christ. As victors, we must be willing to love one another.

"As God's chosen people, holy and dearly loved, clothe yourselves with compassion, kindness, humility, gentleness and patience. Bear with each other and forgive whatever grievances you may have against one another. Forgive as the Lord forgave you. And over all these virtues put on love, which binds them all together in perfect unity" (Colossians 3:12–14).

"You have heard that it was said, 'Love your neighbor and hate your enemy.' But I tell you: Love your enemies and pray for those who persecute you, that you may be sons of your Father in heaven. He causes his sun to rise on the evil and the good, and sends rain on the righteous and the unrighteous. If you love those who love you, what reward will you get? Are not even the tax collectors doing that? . . . Do not even pagans do that?" (Matthew 5:43–47).

People are not the enemy. They are God's children, even though many are misguided in their loyalty and need further training in what this battle is all about and which side they belong on. The only enemy we are out to destroy is the devil. In this battle it is our duty to rip God's kids out of the devil's grasp and pull them to safety. Our job as soldiers is to have the attitude of a soldier: Leave no man behind. When Jesus comes to gather His troops and take us home, let's make sure we all go.

Jesus told a parable about a lost sheep. There were a hundred sheep in the shepherd's flock, and the shepherd knew every one of them by name. One night, one of those precious sheep was lost. The shepherd left the ninety-nine and went out in search of the one that was lost. When he found him, there was great rejoicing, for the shepherd was not willing to lose even one.

Our victory is already sure. Let's go out there and fight this battle together. Let's not settle for a 99 percent success rate. Let's not be willing to lose even one.

There are additional issues to deal with concerning forgiveness. One of the issues I faced was whether I had to forgive if my trespassers weren't sorry for what they had done. If they didn't repent, I didn't have to forgive them, right? Wrong!

I have to be willing to forgive them whether they have asked for forgiveness or not. The point is that God is willing to forgive them. He stands at the ready to accept their repentance. That repentance is not for me. It's for the salvation of the sinner, and that's between God and the sinner. I have to be willing to forgive others if God is to forgive me.

Another issue is that forgiveness is not the same as trust. Just because I forgave Billy and Ray doesn't mean that I am going to fling open prison doors and welcome them into my home. First of all, justice demands that they serve their sentence whether they are sorry or not. When we do something wrong, even if we seek forgiveness, there may be consequences to our actions.

Billy and Ray committed a crime, and the consequence of that crime is imprisonment. I have every right to demand justice even after I forgive them for what they did. Forgiveness doesn't remove those consequences.

Second, even if they are sorry, there's no guarantee that they have changed completely and will not try to hurt me again. Forgiving them doesn't mean that I have to put myself back in harm's way. I live 1,500 miles from the prison for a reason. I don't want to be anywhere near there when they open those prison doors.

There's a series of Peanuts cartoons about Lucy tempting Charlie Brown to kick the football. Every time he makes a run at it to kick it, she moves the ball, and Charlie Brown lands flat on his back. Every time, Lucy promises she won't move it this time, but every time she does, and Charlie Brown lands flat on his back all over again.

Forgiveness doesn't mean we have to keep on taking the abuse of another. Just because people say they are sorry doesn't mean they've repented of their ways and changed. If someone has habitually abused us, more likely than not our victimizer will keep on victimizing us if we let him or her. And we keep being a victim instead of a victor. It's up to us to break the cycle because they won't. It's our choice. We do not have to be like Charlie Brown.

Sometimes forgiveness means forgiving ourselves. Sometimes tragedy strikes, and we blame ourselves for how or why it happened. Sometimes that guilt is justified; sometimes it's not.

Mark Harris certainly had to deal with this kind of guilt. He had invited Tammy to Springerville to spend time with her, to get to know her better, to propose to her, and spend the rest of his life with her. He saw a beautiful future before him. And then he lit that match—and their lives were changed forever.

It certainly wasn't intentional. He was only lighting the furnace so the building would be warm before the children started coming in for Sabbath School. His motives were pure.

If only he'd been more careful. If only he'd recognized that the propane gas had been building up in the room and would head straight for the door that Tammy had just come through and was even now standing in front of. If only he had told her to wait outside while he lit that match. But that's not what happened, and there is nothing that can ever be done to undo the damage of that one lighted match. Living with that kind of guilt can be devastating.

The hardest part of the tragedy for Mark was having to watch someone he loved suffer because of something he did. Mark would willingly have taken Tammy's pain if it could have relieved her suffering. But there was nothing he could do to change any of it. He was totally helpless. He could not love her enough to heal her. All he could do was cope with it as best he could to honor their relationship. He had to be strong for Tammy, even when his heart was breaking.

Tammy never blamed Mark for the accident. Only Mark blamed Mark, and Mark needed to learn to forgive himself. If we can recognize that we're all sinners in need of repentance, to the point that we can actually forgive others who have trespassed against us, then we have to be willing to forgive ourselves as well. We are just as human as the next guy. But if God can forgive us when we repent, then so can we.

We will never stand as victors if we can't forgive ourselves. Guilt just isn't part of the uniform. Whatever you have done in the past, lay it at the Savior's feet and know that it is all taken care of. You're salvation is sure.

Romans 4:7, 8, tell us: " 'Blessed are they whose transgressions are forgiven, whose sins are covered. Blessed is the man whose sin the Lord will never count against him.' "

MY RESOLUTION

I may not accomplish it all today, but I have to face the fact that even I am in need of forgiveness. If God is to forgive my sins, I have to be willing to forgive those who have trespassed against me. I will ask God to help me understand how I can forgive.

CHAPTER 16
UNITED WE STAND

*If you have any encouragement from being united with Christ,
if any comfort from his love, if any fellowship with the Spirit,
if any tenderness and compassion, then make my joy complete by being
like-minded, having the same love, being one in spirit and purpose. Do
nothing out of selfish ambition or vain conceit, but in humility consider
others better than yourselves. Each of you should look not only to your
own interests, but also to the interests of others. Your attitude
should be the same as that of Christ Jesus (Philippians 2:1–5).*

Our time together has almost come to an end. I hope the information on these pages has empowered you as much as it has me. None of us are alone out there. But it takes getting out of our own fortresses to find that out. We are a multitude of victims, but we don't have to stay that way.

Living the life of a victor is a choice that we make every moment of our lives. It's an allegiance, really, that we will unite as one people under God, indivisible, with liberty and justice for all. Yeah, I know that sounds a lot like our nation's pledge. I admit I stole the lines. But think about that.

If we all pledge our allegiance to God and refuse to be divided no matter what anybody throws at us, if we strive to make sure every man, woman, and child is treated with equal respect and equal rights, then think about what that would do to the devil's cause. We would break him!

The victor's goal is not just to prepare personally for that great day of the Second Coming. It starts out that way. But as we grow, as we develop the characters that Christ wants us to have, we start looking at other people. We begin caring about our wounded brothers and sisters, and we start looking for ways to help them be victors, too.

Understanding the character that God wants us to develop and why it is so important helps us to get a grip on why we need to make the effort, to pay attention to the lessons, and to make a change. It's all too easy to slip into old habits. The habits of a victim are no different, especially when we find ourselves in old territory or faced with reminders of our scars. That's going to happen, but that doesn't mean we're defeated.

When I learned to roller skate, I fell down a lot! You can't roller skate on mattresses. You have to learn on concrete. Falling hurts. But if you're going to master those skates, you must get back up again, starting on all fours if you have to, grab the rail, and push off once more. Use as many props as you need, but don't give up. There's still time to learn. When Jesus comes, if we've tried our hardest, He'll be satisfied with our progress. In heaven, we'll all be master skaters.

More than anything else in the world, I would like to have raised my children to adulthood. But through their loss, I have come to know God and where I stand in the bigger scheme of things. Before the kids were killed, I didn't even know there was a bigger battle. Even if I knew about a battle, I had nothing at stake that I knew of. Now I fight for my family—for God's family—because I am determined to be part of the victory.

Too often we find ourselves soldiers in that unseen war. We have to be strong enough to stand up and say, "Satan can hurt me, step all over me, even take away everything that is precious to me. But he will not defeat me, and he cannot deprive me of my salvation."

Life isn't always fair. But God promises to be with us in our suffering, and He has made a way for us to be with Him in a place where there will be no more death nor sorrow nor sighing nor crying nor any more pain. God does not want to repeat earth's history of heartache any more than we do. He longs to put an end to the chaos and draw His children under His wings.

If we realize that our suffering actually serves a purpose, that it is a vital part of perfecting our characters to fit us for heaven, it's a whole lot easier to focus on being overcomers. And those of us who have suffered most and endured in His name will be the greatest witnesses to the universe against Satan's independent government of sin.

Each of us must experience the pain personally to understand the battle. Then God's people will long for the destruction of sin and a life free of it. Through our suffering, we will have seen the horrible side of sin and reject the temptations and pleasures derived from it. And when we stand before God's throne, we will sing a new song that no one who hasn't gone through trials can sing.

It's been more than twenty-six years since we buried the kids. It took time, but George and I have developed a deep and trusting relationship with God. We try to focus on what God has done for us, and what He continues to do, as we wait for His coming.

Our three living children are adults and on their own. Not one of them is attending church right now, and we pray that God will do whatever it takes to make them realize their need of a Savior. With that prayer comes the risk that they, too, may have to suffer to understand. My eyes are focused on the bigger picture, and I just want them to be ready when He comes. I am willing to suffer heartache with them if that's what it takes to bring them back to a relationship with God.

We can't undo the past. But at some point we have to be willing to lay down the baggage we've been packing around and resume our journey toward home. Parts of our past have permanent results from which we will never be free on this earth. But we can stand victorious even over those parts.

I will not get my children back in this lifetime. And yet I have not lost them. I will be with them again. God Himself told me that in a motel room more than twenty-five years ago, and I believe that God will do what He says He will.

That doesn't give me back what I lost in this life. But in light of eternity, we begin to catch a glimpse of recovering what we lost. One day Jesus will return; He has promised it.

I've accepted the fact that I'll never get over losing my children in this life. I'll never get over the fact that they were robbed of their lives here on earth. They could have had this life *and* eternal life, but there is nothing we can do to restore the lives they've lost here or the children and the grandchildren they might have had if they'd been given the opportunity to live.

My husband is now in his late sixties, and his goal is to hold a grandchild. Our loss cannot be numbered, and our grieving will not be completely over until Jesus comes in the clouds to make our family whole again.

But we're not defeated, because He is coming! He's going to undo the tragedy. In spite of all that we have lost, in light of eternity, everything's all right. We are like gold tried in the fire, and when Jesus comes we are going to shine in His kingdom. We are going to stand as witnesses to His victory!

As we look back on 6,000 years of pain and suffering, we wonder if it will ever be over. We wonder if we'll ever see that little cloud that heralds His coming. We wonder if we'll ever gaze on those pearly gates and enter those glorious mansions that He left to prepare for us almost 2,000 years ago.

All the signs tell us that it won't be much longer. If we can just hang in there a little while longer, He'll be back to make everything that was all wrong in our lives all right again. If we can stand as witnesses to His strength, His patience, and His love in all circumstances on earth, we will stand before the King of the universe and hear the words, "Well done, My good and faithful servant. Enter the kingdom that has been prepared for you."

And when we see all that lies before us to enjoy from now through all eternity, we will look back on our trials and say, "Heaven was cheap enough."

MY RESOLUTION

By the grace of God I will have the faith to patiently endure all things. I will wait upon Him, knowing that my salvation is almost here. I will wear God's armor with humility, compassion, obedience, and love. I will do no harm to my brothers and sisters in Christ. Rather, I will fight to pull them out of Satan's grasp so that we leave no soldier behind. The victory is ours!

IF YOU ENJOYED THIS BOOK,
YOU'LL ENJOY THESE ALSO:

Battered to Blessed: My Personal Journey

Brenda Walsh with *Kay D. Rizzo*. To look at "Miss Brenda" today singing gospel music or hosting her children's TV program on 3ABN, you'd never know the horrors of domestic violence that she once endured. *Battered to Blessed* is Brenda Walsh's amazing journey from pain to peace, and to loving again, trusting again, and living a whole new life of incredible joy in Jesus!

0-8163-2067-5. Paperback.

US$14.99, Can$22.49.

United by Tragedy

David Wilkins with Cecil Murphey. When Swissair Flight 111 crashed in the ocean on September 2, 1998, the world of Dr. David Wilkins and his wife Janet—like the flight their son had taken—came crashing to a halt. Their painful journey would lead them to a rocky Nova Scotia coastline and to a reevaluation of all they had ever believed.

0-8163-1980-4. Paperback.

US$12.99, Can$19.49.

Set Free

Michael and Amber Harris with *James Ponder. Set Free* is more than a story about drug abuse, a tragic accident, and paralysis. It's an unforgettable love story about a spiritually broken man, a physically broken woman, and an all-powerful, all-loving God who specializes in mending broken people. It is virtually impossible to read this story without being moved first to tears, and then moved to embrace and praise the God who makes us all "free indeed."

0-8163-2039-X. Paperback.

US$12.99, Can$19.49.

Order from your ABC by calling **1-800-765-6955**, or get online and shop our virtual store at **www.AdventistBookCenter.com**.

- Read a chapter from your favorite book
- Order online
- Sign up for email notices on new products

Prices subject to change without notice.